C000099083

Education:

PUTTING THE RECORD STRAIGHT

Various Authors

Network Educational Press Ltd

Network Educational Press Ltd
PO Box 635
Stafford
ST17 OJR

First Published 1992
© Copyright Network Educational Press Ltd

ISBN 1 85539 011 6

Bound in Great Britain by Redwood Press Ltd, Pegasus Way, Bowerhill, Melksham, Wiltshire.

Acknowledgements

The publishers would like to thank all the contributors for agreeing to work to impossible deadlines. We are grateful to UCCA statistical supplements for their advice and to HMSO and the NCPTA for allowing us to use extracts from their publications.

CONTENTS

PERSONAL PROFILES OF THE CONTRIBUTORS

Professor Paul Black

Paul Black, Professor of Science Education at King's College, London, was Chairman of the Task Group on Assessment and Testing (1987-1988) and Deputy Chairman of the National Curriculum Council (1988-1991). He began his career teaching physics at Birmingham University where he became Professor. He is a member of the International Commission for Physics Education and a consultant to the OECD, the World Bank and to the US National Science Foundation.

Professor Eric Bolton CB

Eric Bolton taught English in secondary schools, lectured in teaching training and was a local education authority inspector of schools before becoming one of Her Majesty's Inspectors of Schools (HMI) in 1973. He served in the national inspectorate (HMI) for 19 years. From 1983 to 1991 he was the Head of the Inspectorate as Her Majesty's Senior Chief Inspector of Schools. Since his retirement from that post in 1991 he has been Professor for Teacher Education at London University's Institute of Education.

Professor Brian Cox

Brian Cox, who was Chairman of the National Curriculum Working Group on English, is John Edward Taylor Professor of English Literature at Manchester University. He has taught at the University of California at Berkeley, and was Pro-Vice Chancellor of Manchester University, 1987-1991. He is co-editor of *Critical Quarterly.*

Arthur De Caux

A Jerseyman and former Head of Modern Languages, Arthur De Caux has been Senior Assistant Secretary dealing with educational matters for the National Association of Head Teachers (NAHT) since 1982. In that capacity he has wrestled with the Education Reform Act in all its parts both seriously, in gathering and writing the Association's views and responses, and humorously, in trenchant after-dinner speeches.

Michael Duffy

Michael Duffy was Head of Evesham High School 1970-1980, and from 1980 became Head of King Edward VI School, Morpeth - a 13-18 Community High School. He is a former President of the Secondary Heads Association and is an author, journalist and speaker in the cause of state education.

Professor Duncan Graham CBE

After teaching, Professor Graham became County Education Officer for Suffolk in 1979. He served on the Burnham Committee on Teachers' Pay and as Chairman of two National Working Parties on Mathematics and Teacher Appraisal. From 1987 to 1988 he was Chief Executive of Humberside County Council, and from 1988 to 1991 Chairman and Chief Executive of the National Curriculum Council. He is now an author, consultant and visiting Professor at the University of Manchester School of Education.

Dr Chris Husbands

Chris Husbands is a lecturer in the School of Education at the University of East Anglia and is a member of the Education Committee and Council of the Historical Association. He previously taught in comprehensive schools in London, Norwich and Hertfordshire.

Louise Kidd BSc M Ed

Louise Kidd had 18 years experience in 11-18 comprehensive schools in Glasgow, Manchester and Preston. She held posts at Deputy Head and Vice Principal level and since 1989 has been Principal of Rutland Sixth Form College. She has served on many educational committees and is currently President of the Secondary Heads Association (1992).

Chris Lowe CBE

Chris Lowe is Head of Prince William School, Oundle, Northamptonshire. He is a past President of the Secondary Heads Association and is currently President of the European Secondary Heads Association.

Michael Marland CBE MA FRSA

Michael Marland is one of the country's most experienced Headteachers, having been head of Woodberry Down throughout the seventies. He founded London's largest school in 1980: North Westminster Community School. He is Honorary Professor of Education at Warwick University, and has lectured widely in this country and abroad. As General Editor of Longman Imprint Books he has pioneered the broadening of the range of modern literature for students. His major contribution to school management has been through his editorship of the Heinemann School Management Series.

The Rev. Dominic Milroy OSB

Father Dominic Milroy was educated at Ampleforth College. He joined the monastery as a Benedictine monk in 1950, and went up to St Benet's Hall, Oxford (1st Class Hons. Modern Languages). He returned to teach at Ampleforth, and became Head of Modern Languages in 1963, and a Housemaster in 1964. In 1974 he went to Rome as Prior of San Anselmo - the Benedictine College. He became Headmaster of Ampleforth College in 1980 and retires at the end of 1992. He is Chairman of the Headmasters' Conference (1992), and Chairman-elect of the Conference of Catholic Secondary Schools and Colleges.

Margaret Murray

Margaret Murray has been Head of the CBI's Education Policy Group since 1989. Before that she had a varied career in teaching.

Joan Sallis

Joan Sallis has never been professionally involved in education but as a campaigning writer she is widely respected at all levels of the system. In her campaign work she has been involved in many organisations but, as she says, 'While others have had my head and my legs it is the Campaign for State Education which has my heart'. She has been involved in education both as parent and a governor and was a parent member of the Taylor Committee on School Government in 1977. She is currently heavily involved in the training and support of school governors. She is on the BBC's Educational Brodcasting Council and writes a weekly agony column for governors in *The Times Educational Supplement.*

Professor John Tomlinson

John Tomlinson has been Director of the Institute of Education at the University of Warwick since January 1985, and was Director of Education for Cheshire 1972-84. He was founder Chairman of the Further Education Unit 1976-78, Chairman of the Schools Council 1978-82, President of the Society of Education Officers 1982-93 and Chairman of the Council of the Royal Society of Arts 1989-91. He is Chairman of the newly formed General Teaching Council for England and Wales.

Philip Waterhouse

Philip Waterhouse is nationally known and respected as a leading authority on flexible learning, supported self-study and resource-based learning. He is a former Headteacher of two schools, and Director of the Avon Resources for Learning Development Unit. From 1981 to 1989 he led the CET supported self-study project and until his retirement in 1991 was an educational consultant, working with hundreds of schools and LEAs.

Professor Ted Wragg

Ted Wragg is the Director of the School of Education at Exeter University. He is the author of several books on primary education, and directed together with Neville Bennett, The Leverhulme Primary Project. He also teaches regularly in primary schools. He writes a regular column in *The Times Educational Supplement.*

INTRODUCTION

*Paul Black, Professor of Science Education, King's College, London,
and former Chairman of the Task Group on Assessment and Testing*

1. Bogeyman thinking in educational policy

The concern that has led many distinguished authors to contribute to this
book is that the National Curriculum is in danger of being changed from a
means for improvement to an instrument for regression. A striking feature of
this development is that the quality of the debate and thinking that has been
informing the shifts in policy is alarmingly low.

One characteristic of the weak thinking is the 'bogeymen' approach. A
group or a trend is identified - the 'educational establishment' or 'woolly
left-wing thinking' - and then any idea, any criticism, any difficulty, is
dismissed by being ascribed to the bogey, so that it is not necessary to think
seriously about it. The chapters by Philip Waterhouse and Ted Wragg both
illustrate how the 'progressive education' bogey has diverted attention from
the real issues about classroom teaching.

A second characteristic is the neglect of evidence. Sweeping claims are
made and repeated so often that the public come to accept them as self-
evident truths. The outstanding example is the claim that standards have
fallen. Such a claim cannot be supported by any review of the extensive
evidence that such a sweeping generalisation must embrace. Those who do
support it usually select one or two pieces of the evidence and neglect the
rest. Both Louise Kidd and Duncan Graham present evidence and
arguments in their chapters to show how standards have been rising.

Another example is the claim that 'progressive child-centred' methods have
done a great deal of harm. Those who broadcast this assertion neglect the
evidence, which Eric Bolton surveys in his chapter, that by any definition of
that vague phrase, there is very little use of 'progressive' methods in our
schools.

A third characteristic is the over-simplification of issues, which often leads to
a naïve polarisation. The debate about teaching methods is reduced to a
choice between the didactic and the informal - a polarisation which makes
about as much sense as telling an unhealthy person to choose between
improving diet and taking more exercise. Arthur de Caux explains how
sensible debates, about reading and about children's achievements at Key

Stage One, have been overwhelmed by a frenetic desire to simplify the issues in order to dramatise them, so that they are almost inevitably misrepresented. A similar over-simplification characterises the arguments about the history curriculum that Chris Husbands describes.

A fourth characteristic is to attack *theory*. There are of course good theories and bad, theories which are grounded in evidence and theories which ignore realities. Many of the oft-despised 'academics' in education have spent their lives trying to improve theory by demanding a meaningful relation to practice. Those who dismiss such work as 'mere' theory are inevitably doing so from a theoretical standpoint of their own - although they often hide behind the smoke-screen of 'common sense'. This smoke-screen must be blown away and the underlying theoretical assumptions exposed to critical scrutiny.

One of the purposes of this book is to provide such scrutiny. Current policies are based on a set of assumptions, notably that a market economy approach is the best way to improve the work of schools, with the corollary that the support structure that LEAs have provided for schools had best be removed. Joan Sallis, John Tomlinson and Dominic Milroy all call in question these assumptions. A similar assumption is that the curriculum is best thought of as a collection of subjects with no need for an overall theory or set of principles. Ted Wragg's chapter illustrates how this position has to be abandoned if we are to find a principled way of restructuring the primary curriculum in order to overcome the mounting crisis of overload that teachers are facing.

Education is a complex matter. To reduce debate about it to simplistic slogans and unjustified assertions is to risk making grave errors. Bogeymen may serve to frighten a child, but they are an obstacle to the development of the adult.

2. Nostalgia as a guide to policy

Outside education, there is no field of public policy where it is seriously argued that we need to return to the practices of the past. Anyone who argued that motorways were an error and that we should return to three-lane A-roads, or that modern anaesthetics were the invention of academic theorists and that we should go back to good old chloroform, would be laughed out of court.

We do face such arguments in education. A return to traditional didactic teaching, a return to traditional testing, a return to O Level, are all on the agenda. Such regression cannot of course be dismissed simply because it is regression. It can be dismissed if it is clear either that the old methods never served our purposes, or that the mores and needs of society are now very different. In education, both of these arguments hold.

We need a vast increase in the proportions of highly trained young people; we need them to be trained to be capable and flexible in quite new ways. Margaret Murray sets out the needs very clearly from the perspective of the CBI. Yet schools have to achieve these targets against a background of profound changes - in media influences, in family life, in expectations of authority. These changes make the teaching of all young people a profoundly different matter from the teaching of the upper-middle-class elite in selective schools twenty years ago. Those trying to fashion a different teaching to meet these new needs sometimes commit excesses, but, as Brian Cox argues in his chapter, the existence of such aberrations is not an argument for a return to outdated and irrelevant approaches in the face of serious professional advice.

Yet it seems that many politicians are driven by nostalgia. Many of them received an education which they enjoyed and from which they derived great profit. What they do not seem to understand is that the experience that their minority enjoyed will not work with the majority of young people today. Furthermore, it would not meet the needs of our society even if it worked.

3. The sad case of assessment

The development of the policy for national assessment seems to be a sadly typical example of the development of the National Curriculum. The government's own Task Group on Assessment and Testing (TGAT) produced recommendations which were welcomed widely and which the government broadly accepted. In subsequent developments, most of the TGAT principles have been abandoned.

The TGAT emphasis on the importance of supporting and enhancing teachers' own assessments of pupils was never understood. Some ministers, even now, still say that they agree that such assessments are of great importance in improving pupils' learning. However, they have not committed substantial resources to improving classroom assessment, and they have decided that teachers' judgements should have only a minor role in the national assessment procedures.

Following this decision, the Prime Minister declared that there was too much teacher assessment; this declaration led to action to reverse one of the most positive developments of GCSE - the development of coursework as a main method of assessment for public certificate examinations. The declaration was not preceded by any public debate or complaint, and to this day the public has not been told from where the Prime Minister got the idea for this particular initiative. It seems as if it arose out of criticisms of the reliability of teachers' assessments and of the fairness of the practices used in the production of coursework in schools.

Of course, it is necessary to look critically at the methods used to assure comparability of standards across different schools and to monitor the fairness of procedures. Unfavourable anecdotes have been quoted, but no substantial body of evidence has been produced - and none was commissioned before the decision was imposed. As a way of conducting public policy this is quite staggering - it is as if a few laymen had complained to the Prime Minister that aspirin gave them nausea and he had therefore declared that it should be a banned drug without recourse to any systematic review and debate about the effects and value of aspirin.

However, there is more at issue here. Michael Duffy and Chris Lowe both explain the fundamental improvements that the GCSE has brought about, so making it clear that to destroy its distinctive features now is to drive us further away from Margaret Murray's targets. More specifically, Michael Marland's chapter discusses the ways in which emphasis on assessed coursework has improved the learning of pupils. Coursework gives more realistic targets than written examinations provide, enhances motivation to serious study and raises the expectations of many pupils. This improvement in learning should be the central feature of the debate. Such improvements are precious, and associated difficulties with assessment should therefore be tackled to clear away any threats to their achievement. Here, as elsewhere, not only have the assessment issues been addressed in a superficial way, but the issues about more effective learning, which assessment ought to support, appear to have been completely ignored.

The distrust of teachers' assessment has seriously weakened the development of the National Curriculum. Teachers are required to keep assessment records and to report their results, but the message to them is clear - your efforts are not to be trusted. This would be galling even if there were good alternative means of external assessment - but there are not. Here the nostalgia and the simplistic thinking enter to degrade public policy.

It is seriously believed - for example, for science at Key Stage Three - that a three-hour written test will serve to establish the level of a pupil in each of three separate attainment targets. It is further believed that this three-hour episode will give a more trustworthy result than can be produced by the teachers who have been teaching that pupil for three years.

No one with expert knowledge about the reliability and validity of written tests could take such a proposition seriously. The results will be unreliable, so they might harm individual pupils unless parents and schools decide to take little notice of them. Worse than this, the pressures on teachers to produce good results in such tests will lead them to drill pupils for them, which means learning by heart the atomised bits of knowledge that any such short tests are reduced to rewarding. The reform goals, of providing a rigorous and high-quality education for all pupils, are thus subverted by policy makers who are suspicious of all new methods, who have never understood the serious limitations of the old ones, and who emphasise assessment as an end in itself without reference to the way it affects teaching and learning.

Of course, again, there are some real bogeymen, who oppose such tests because they are against all forms of assessment and do not believe in the rights and needs of both the public and of pupils themselves to good-quality evaluation of the outcomes of school learning. Because of this minority, the serious critics, who are seriously technical and want to contribute to better assessment, are dismissed - they are seen as bogeymen. Perhaps here we need to start all over again, as Duncan Graham advocates in suggesting that schools should be supported and validated as assessors and then given full responsibility for all National Curriculum assessments, at least up to age 16.

4. Encouraging success

As Margaret Murray emphasises in her chapter, future society needs young people who will be autonomous, capable of taking decisions, well informed and highly skilled. Such targets have to be attained by the great majority of young people, not just by that minority who succeed in narrowly academic pursuits. Traditional education contributed very little to the achievement of this target, even whilst, with selected elite groups, its teaching task was relatively easy. Traditional methods, whilst having a particular contribution to make, cannot on their own be adequate to the task.

Yet schools have been making great progress in helping an ever-increasing proportion of their pupils to achieve educational success. The chapters by Chris Lowe, Louise Kidd and Michael Duffy all support this view. They also argue that, at the same time, the quality of the achievements has been changing in the direction that our society needs. My own examples here are the developments in the teaching of practical science and practical mathematics to all and the emerging implementation of the quite new educational goals set out in National Curriculum Design and Technology. A further example is TVEI, to which I refer below.

What is needed now? The first need is that these achievements be recognised, and that some praise and celebration replace the constant denigration that the media and some politicians appear too ready to provide. Teachers' morale needs a boost, not a boot.

Secondly, there needs to be a different degree of awareness of the realities of educational change. It is not possible to mandate the most important aspect of school teaching, the interactions in the classroom. Reform prescriptions can be handed down to teachers, but unless they can translate the new mandates into their own classroom action, the reforms will not happen. Teachers need to be consulted in the formulation of the changes, and they need time and space in which they can adapt the new to their own style. They also need support: one of the most helpful sources is the opportunity to join in dialogue with colleagues and outside experts in order to make sure that they understand the rationale for changes and can share those experiences and insights which can only be forged in the arena of practice.

An outstanding example here is the success of the TVEI scheme. The source of this success is that the scheme sets general targets and offers resources, but leaves schools to formulate their own programmes in their bids to the scheme and leaves to them the responsibility for putting the general aims into practice with the extra resources. The outcome has been an extraordinary flowering of curriculum thinking and implementation - very much in the direction of the very improvements, in technological and practical capability, that many agencies, not least the government, say that they want schools to follow. It is therefore very puzzling that, far from congratulating themselves on the success of their own strategy and building on the lessons that might be learned from it, the politicians and the civil servants appear to have ignored TVEI in the formulation of the National Curriculum plans and in the manner of their implementation.

A third point that follows from the second is that effective change is bound to happen slowly. This is not simply because teachers are conservative or inflexible. It arises because of the complexity of teaching. A vision that is attractive in the abstract can turn out to lead to such unforeseen consequences when translated into practice that it has to be radically reformulated if it is to serve its authors' original aims. There is no substitute for the patient to and fro between principle and practice if a robust and valid change is to be achieved. There are no short cuts.

A new educational formula should be treated rather like a new drug in medicine, taking several years of patient trial before approval for use. The same reason applies in both cases - the system is complex and the side-effects of application cannot be predicted. A corollary in education is that a new measure can produce difficulties when first tried such that, in its first trial, the innovation can seem to be making things worse. It is only when practice has been adapted to work with the innovation, and vice versa, that the potential benefit is realised. The worst strategy is to abandon innovations at the first sight of difficulties, and then to present teachers with new rules just when they are beginning to make sense of putting the old ones into practice.

The above points are not idle theorising on my part. They have all arisen from well-documented research studies in this country and in several others. These studies have tried to follow closely the realities of educational change in schools. Those responsible for changing education might have proceeded with reform measures in more careful ways, ways that would have been both more humane and more effective in achieving their ends, if they had been aware of this evidence. Unfortunately,they were not, and attempts to draw the relevant literature to the attention of politicians are dismissed because those who know about it are the bogeymen. If the evidence were to be taken seriously, it would put governments in a dilemma, because it shows that the time scale for realising effective change is longer than the interval between elections, and far longer than the average time in office of a cabinet minister.

Without drawing on this particular type of evidence, but arguing from long experience and insight, Dominic Milroy's chapter illustrates such issues in a different way. He reminds us powerfully that teachers are our main source of knowledge about how to improve teaching so that it has been absurd to fail to draw out and draw upon that knowledge. He also puts into focus the central role of the teacher, which is to play a critically important role in the developing experience and relationships of the child.

If educational policy were to focus more on the needs, and the many deprivations, of today's children, teachers might be treated with more respect - they are not just the delivery agents for the National Curriculum.

In his book, *'The Audit of War'*, Corelli Barnett shows that one of the sources of this country's long and steady slide into industrial decline was the cult of the practical man in business and industry. Questions of design, of technical innovation, of marketing, of management were best decided by those who had grown up in the business. Academics, those informed by scholarly study of principles and evidence, whether in engineering, or design, or business studies, were mere theorists who could only distract practical men from the real business of production and profit. In consequence, our industries inherited poor practices, outdated products, and an inability to adapt and compete with countries who took technical matters seriously. Education now faces a similar prejudice, but with an additional handicap - those on the shop floor are not listened to either. It is ironic that education is now to suffer because those who have gained control of it have not been well educated about education.

THE QUALITY OF TEACHING

Eric Bolton CB MA, Professor of Teacher Education, University of London, Institute of Education, and Former Senior Chief Inspector of Schools

In the current, bruising debate about quality and standards in our schools, it has become commonplace for those who believe that standards are falling to lay a large part of the blame on '*trendy teachers*'. There is no doubt that the phrase is used pejoratively to imply that teachers have blindly and thoughtlessly followed fashion, and, as a consequence, all kinds of important educational babies are said to have been lost with the bath-water.

At the heart of that accusation is a sharp division of view about the business of teaching. At the one extreme is Charles Dickens's Mr Gradgrind, for whom only facts were important. So important was factual knowledge that in his teaching, and in his life, Gradgrind lost all sight of the importance of understanding and mastery. In his school, of course, the utterly singular insistence on facts led Gradgrind to judge that Cissy Jupe was the only one of his pupils to know absolutely nothing about horses, despite the fact that Cissy lived in and worked in the circus, training and looking after horses.

At the other extreme, to lose all sense of the teacher as knowing things and directing learning leads to the abdication of the teacher and a consequent lack of guidance and standard setting for the pupils. In such circumstances the teacher becomes little more than a facilitator, lightly guiding the discovery and enquiry of the pupils, neither influencing the direction nor the quality of that discovery, nor of those enquiries.

At the extremes, of course, both are, quite simply, *bad teaching.*

Good teaching is as varied as is the number of good teachers in the service, and there are a great number of those. However, whatever its particular style and characteristics, good teaching is necessarily a compromise between the teacher as font of all knowledge and director of all activity, and the teacher as mentor and guide, drawing from the pupil that which they have to give. More of that later. Now I want to return to the question of trendy teachers and teaching, and to examine a little more why that particular accusation is made and what, if any, truth there is in it.

The notion of trendiness in education seems to have its roots in the 'swinging 60s', when there were significant and important changes in British society after the long period of austerity that followed the ending of the Second World War. This is not the place to examine those changes in detail; suffice it to say that society in general, in its institutions and in its personal relationships, began to question long-established practice and to open up and relax in a variety of ways.

Many taboos and proscriptions were re-examined and boundaries broadened or, indeed, ditched all together. Central to that was the emergence of the young; teenagers and young people moved to centre-stage in ways that were quite new. Adult and child relationships changed dramatically, not always for the better, but much of the change was positive, welcomed and lasting. Education was not immune from such changes. Nor could it ever have been so, because schools, to a large extent, reflect the kind of society they serve, rather than set patterns for it. The teachers, pupils, parents and governors who make up the school community are not isolated from the wider community of the village, the town or the country. They bring into schools the influences of those broader and deeper movements of society that have affected them. Centrally, and fundamentally, between the end of the 1950s and the present, our society has undergone a transformation in the way adults regard children, and in the way society regards young people. Education and the relationships between teachers and taught have had no choice but to respond to those changes in a variety of ways.

During the 1960s therefore, much that was going on in education was under scrutiny and subject to change. At such times all kinds of experts, pundits and messiahs appear to point the way for the rest of society to go. Some turn out to be true and sound, others to be ephemeral and unreliable. But the general thrust of the advice, and of the change, in our schools throughout that period was to move the balance of that compromise that constitutes teaching the young, from the Gradgrind end of the spectrum towards one in which the child, and his or her needs, and possibilities, were nearer the centre of concern.

That approach has been called 'child-centred education'. At its silliest, child-centred education set out to leave everything to the child to decide and to determine; children would learn to read when they were 'ready' to read, and would work and play when they felt ready to work and play.

14

A number of educational gurus were prominent in promulgating those ideas. In addition, in the 1960s, the government set up a Committee of Enquiry into Primary Education, because of the amount of change taking place within it. That enquiry was headed by Lady Plowden and became known as the Plowden Committee. In the demonology of the right-wing critics of education in our schools, though not in reality, the Plowden Report features as the document that furthered and promoted child-centred discovery and enquiry-led education. In the opinion of those critics, it hastened the flight away from hard-nosed, factually based education, led and directed by the teacher, into *progressive* sloppiness. The belief that so-called experts and academics were playing a leading role in the education debate led to the notion that teachers, the majority of whom were reasonable people, were being *'led by the nose as asses are'*; that they were adopting without question whatever trendy fashion was being promoted by one or other of the educational gurus.

In that scenario, teachers were led, uncomplainingly and unconsciously, into sloppy, soft-centred and *'progressive'* forms of teaching and learning, in which concerns about quality and excellence, rigour of study and qualities such as perseverance were ditched.

Just how true or not is that scenario? It is important to know because, if what is said to have happened *has* happened, our education service and the quality of teaching are in a sorry state. It is also vital to know because, if trendy teaching is a major cause of our educational shortcomings, we know what to set right in order to remedy matters.

For some twenty years of my working life I was privileged to do a job that gave me access to hundreds of schools, and to thousands of classrooms across the country. It also gave me access to thousands upon thousands of no-axe-to-grind, inspection-based judgements and descriptions of education produced by Her Majesty's Inspectors of Schools (HMI). The job of that body of men and women was to inform the government of the day about the state of the education service, and to make those judgements known to the education service in particular, and the public more generally.

In commenting on the state of education, HMI's central concern was always with the standards of the learning being achieved by the pupils. Many factors affect standards of learning but, without doubt, the characteristic most closely associated with high standards of learning is high-quality teaching.

Consequently, a great deal of what HMI had to say about standards of learning in our schools commented, in some detail, on the quality of teaching, and upon teaching styles, methodologies, attitudes, values and effectiveness.

I would be hard put to it, out of that welter of data and evidence, to say which, if any, single issue characterises teaching in our schools, unless it is that the vast majority of teachers are firmly committed to doing the best they possibly can for their pupils. More particularly, there emerges a picture of tremendous variation and variety, shot through with a strong and durable vein of common sense. Consequently, the evidence of all that national inspection directly contradicts the claim that throughout the 1970s teachers in England blindly followed trends and fashion, and in doing so gave up their traditional practices and methodologies.

There is no doubt that in schools, as elsewhere in society, relationships between adults and children have become more informal and relaxed. Teachers, like lawyers, doctors, parents and others, no longer automatically receive respect simply by holding a particular position: they have to earn it. But, leaving aside those major societal changes, much teaching, rather than swinging wildly, buffeted by the winds of fashion and change, remains stubbornly unchanged and unimpressed by loud and fashionable voices claiming to have discovered the way to do things.

A good example to illustrate my point is that of the teaching of reading in our primary schools. Periodically, we experience a crisis of conscience and belief in the teaching of reading in our schools. We are going through one now. At such times it is often claimed that schools and teachers have given up old and well-tried ways and have plumped for a new, fashionable approach. In fact, the evidence shows that schools and teachers who adopt a one-track approach to the teaching of reading, whether it is phonics and nothing else, or real books and nothing else, achieve lower standards of reading than similar schools using a mix of methods and styles.

The vast majority of heads and teachers in our primary schools, on the basis of observation of, and detailed, day-to-day involvement in teaching, know that the common-sense and straight-forward way to teach reading is to use, and to mix together, a variety of approaches and styles. They do that to satisfy not only the different needs of the subject matter itself, but also to appeal to, and motivate, groups of children characterised by variety and diversity in age, competence, ability, interest and maturity.

The evidence of inspection is that poor standards of learning are more commonly associated with over-direction by teachers, rather than with teachers opting out and allowing the pupils to set the style and pace of learning. Time and again in HMI reports, whether concerning bright or not so bright children, older or younger pupils, academic or practical lessons, the criticism is that the teachers over-direct, over-determine and unduly narrow the scope and focus of what is being studied, or undertaken, with the consequence that the achievements of the pupils are limited and depressed.

When Inspectors makes such judgements they do not have in mind a blue-print for the style of teaching they think everyone should adopt. They compare what they see in any particular instance with what they have already seen, as Inspectors, in hundreds of similar schools and classrooms elsewhere. They are not dangling an impossible dream before politicians, teachers or parents, but are saying, quite simply, that more and better could be achieved because they have seen, in very similar situations to this one, more and better being achieved. Furthermore, the Inspectors set out to show which characteristics are affecting standards of learning, for good or ill.

If, as is claimed by the critics of our schools, large proportions of teachers had trendily followed the latest fashions, the most common criticisms arising from Inspectors' reports about the standards being achieved would be that teachers had lost an important balance in their methodology; were neither expecting, nor, insisting on, high standards, and were failing to give the lead and direction to learning that, as teachers, they ought to give.

There are examples where these criticisms apply. But such cases do not constitute any great proportion. The far more frequent criticism of teaching leading to pupils achieving less than they ought, is of teachers being over-directive, unduly concerned with factual learning at the expense of understanding and mastery of subject matter, and failing to extend and challenge pupils as they should. In fact, our biggest failing in education, as a country, is that we do not draw out and capitalise upon the qualities and talents of the majority of ordinary people and, through their achievement, understanding and mastery, give them any sense of educational success.

Far from having an education service full of trendy teachers led, willy-nilly, this way and that by experts and gurus (the 'Educational Mafia'), we have a teaching profession that is essentially cautious and conservative: a profession that is highly suspicious of claims from within or without its ranks that there is a particular, fool-proof way of doing things. Teachers are too close to the actual, day-to-day complexity of classrooms, and to the variability of people and pupils, to be anything else but pragmatic and commonsensical in their thinking and actions.

In fact, that conservatism is one of the great problems facing educational change and reform. It is extremely difficult to bring about change, even in quite small things in education, even where all the evidence is that what is being sought actually works. The Americans are much concerned with the poor state of much of their public education service. In seeking to bring about improvement they produced, some years ago, a remarkable pamphlet entitled '*What Works*'. That pamphlet simply and straight-forwardly illustrates a range of approaches, methodologies, teaching styles, across various subjects, as well as organisational and management techniques, that experience has shown to work. They work in that they deliver high standards of pupil application and learning. The question the pamphlet poses is that, if we all know what works, and if there is no great problem or secret about making it work, why doesn't everybody do it? It was exactly that question, in relation to a number of things known to work, that informed much of the thinking in the national criteria for the GCSE examination, and, later, the development of attainment targets and programmes of study built into the National Curriculum.

There are real challenges and shortcomings in our education service, and in the standards it achieves and expects, that need to be faced. We do need to tackle them, and, to some extent, we are doing so. To claim, however, that our problems are as they are largely because of trendy teachers being misled by a trendy education establishment is so misguided as to be totally counter-productive.

The trouble with debates that are posited upon such notions as 'trendy teaching' is that they are informed and led by people who seem to believe in the conspiracy theory of history. They act as if any complex and complicated situation can be reduced to the simplicity of melodrama. All that is needed is to find the villain, the wicked squire, remove him, and all will be well. If only the world was like that. If only the bad guys always wore black hats, and the good guys white hats. If only people could be led in this direction, or that, as simply and as easily as the conspiracy theorist would have it. If all that were true, we would have no difficulties. Once we had agreed what we wanted our education service to be like, we could simply get everybody to follow us, and what was known to work would become a reality.

But it isn't like that. Life is much more complex, and so are our teachers, schools, classrooms and education systems. During the 1930s depression in America a famous labour leader came to address a huge rally of people, many of whom were out of work. As he entered and acknowledged the applause, he opened his speech by saying: *'I have not come to lead you out of the wilderness. If I can lead you out, then the next man who comes along can lead you right back in again.'*

That is the truth of the matter. Not only is it not desirable for people to be led, or to be persuaded to be led, by the nose, in reality it is not possible for any length of time, nor for all the people. It has certainly not happened to the bulk of teachers in our schools. On the contrary, what they are pressing for most, at present, is a deal more clarity about where the nation thinks its education service should go and, in deciding that, a proper and constructive dialogue between all with an interest, including teachers and politicians, about how we might get there.

That dialogue, if it is to be any good at all in its outcomes, had better deal with the real complexity of things, and not with slogans such as 'trendy teachers' and the 'Educational Mafia'.

THE TEACHING OF ENGLISH

Brian Cox, Professor of English Literature, Manchester University and former Chairman of the National Curriculum English Working Group

When I was at school in the 1930s and 1940s, English was often taught badly. After the outbreak of war in 1939 the Army found that many conscripts were illiterate. In 1947, when I was enlisted into the Royal Army Education Corps, we were told that one-third of the conscripts were semi-literate. This meant they couldn't read the firearm instructions and so needed to be told about safety regulations. In my autobiography, *The Great Betrayal*, I describe how I taught illiterates in the Army in 1948. I had received no training on how to teach reading, and soon discovered that to succeed one needs professional skills. I was able to give little help to my pupils.

The teaching methods in the schools in the 1930s depended heavily on rote learning, and on boring exercises such as parsing and clause analysis. The clever children, of course, advanced quickly in their reading and writing skills, as they usually do whatever the quality of the teaching. They were selected at a very early age and placed in an 'A' stream. Many of these children are now in their sixties, and look back with nostalgia to those golden, far-off days. They forget that less able children fared badly under this system, and received little individual attention. In those days the lower streams were usually allocated to the less experienced teachers. When I left the Army I spent four months as an untrained supply teacher in a secondary modern school at Immingham in South Humberside. Although I had no qualifications, I was asked to teach reading to a group of illiterate 13-year-olds. I was a complete failure, and didn't know how to help them.

In the 1930s and 1940s children were taught rules about the English language which are now recognised as false. A middle-aged teacher told me that when he was at school he was cuffed for writing 'a dilapidated wooden shed'; '*Lapis* means a stone,' proclaimed the teacher, tweaking his ear. 'You foolish boy; you can't call something wooden dilapidated.' As late as the 1960s a professor at Bedford College told his students that 'companion' must be used only for a person with whom one eats (*panis*, with bread, food). These teachers were applying Latin rules to English, and we now realise that this is ridiculous. Children were taught not to begin sentences with 'and' or 'but', and not to end the sentence with a preposition.

They were told not to split the infinitive. For many years now university linguists have been demonstrating that these rules do not apply to the English language.

Great writers such as Byron and D.H. Lawrence split their infinitives. The excellent *Reader's Digest* 'The Right Word at the Right Time' (1986) says that the rule that you must not split the infinitive is 'irrational'. Phrases such as 'to boldly go where no man has gone before' and 'begin to silently hope' are guaranteed to set the pedant's teeth on edge - despite the greater metrical regularity of 'to boldly go' and 'to silently hope'. In a witty entry in his *A Dictionary of Modern English Usage* (revised by Gowers, 1965), Fowler pokes fun at those pedants whose tortuous efforts to avoid split infinitives are deaf to the normal rhythms of English sentences.

Old people get very upset when they are told that the English rules they were taught at school are wrong. The way we write and speak is part of our identity, and it's destabilising to find that modern usage has left us behind. This is why many elderly Conservatives get so emotional about language. Some of these are now in charge of the National Curriculum.

In the 1950s and 1960s good teachers started rejecting these old-fashioned, boring and inaccurate ways of teaching English. Unfortunately some of them went to the other extreme. The pendulum swung too far. Because grammar had been taught badly, they taught no grammar. 'Creative' writing became fashionable, and children were encouraged to express themselves freely without bothering about spelling, punctuation or grammar. Instead of helping children read through structured programmes of work, including use of phonics, some 'progressive' teachers said that reading skills would develop by themselves as long as children were provided with lots of attractive and enjoyable reading materials. In the 1960s many traditional teachers opposed these excesses, and they were proved right. In 1969 I edited the *Black Papers on Education* which attacked these 'free' methods. In 1976 at Ruskin College, Oxford, Lord Callaghan made a famous speech in which he emphasised the need to return to basics, and by 1980 more and more schools were teaching English by using a mix of the best of the traditional and progressive methods.

During the next twelve years the quality of English teaching improved markedly. Teachers, of course, face huge problems in this television age when many children prefer to watch cartoons or play Nintendo instead of applying themselves to the more difficult task of learning to read.

The National Curriculum in English of 1989 reflected what was best in modern approaches to teaching. This is mostly a question of tone and attitude. The new curriculum talked about opportunities and entitlement of pupils, and it did not take a rigid, authoritarian stance. But in terms of content it was more rigorous and demanding than anything published since 1945. It was welcomed by teachers, and in its early stages has been raising standards. There were new approaches to the teaching of grammar and knowledge about language. For the past three years teachers have worked extraordinarily hard to implement these National Curriculum proposals.

National Curriculum English gives due weight to spelling, grammar and handwriting. But instead of the old boring exercises, young children are encouraged to write their own stories, to discuss them with the teacher and their friends, and to improve them, perhaps for printing in a school magazine. In their discussions with the teacher, grammar and knowledge about language can be introduced to help children improve their writing skills. It's no use telling a child a verb is a doing word. The verb 'to be' isn't. What is needed is for children to understand how they can communicate more forcefully if they use active verbs. Teachers are very excited by these new approaches to language, and believe they are the best way of teaching English to children of all abilities. Instead of tedious exercises, children study language in use.

Literature teaching has changed in similar ways. When I was at school we studied Shakespeare and the classics in boring ways which often put children off great literature for life. We spent hours copying down the teacher's notes, and learning them in great detail for tests. Today teachers encourage children to act in scenes from Shakespeare, to watch videos, to argue about themes, to write their own versions of the stories in modern settings.

And so we come to 1992, when some early traditionalists want to impose the old practices of the 1930s on the schools. They attack trendy, progressive teachers for not teaching spelling or Shakespeare. Their rhetoric is appropriate to some bad schools in the 1970s, but not to what is happening in most schools today. During the last three years I have visited many wonderful schools. Teachers understand that there is no one way of teaching reading, and that they must use a variety of methods.

Some children do well when there is much emphasis on phonics; others take less well to this method. The teacher must use his or her professional skills to devise special strategies to help children who are in difficulty. Spelling and grammar are strongly emphasised. Shakespeare is compulsory in the National Curriculum.

Over the past decade, and particularly in the past three years, there has been a steady development in the quality of the teaching of English throughout the system. It is particularly regrettable, therefore, to see the wild and unjustified attacks on the teaching profession indulged by some politicians. It's not surprising that teachers are in despair when ill-informed politicians interfere with their work. At present the morale of teachers is very low. They deserve our complete support.

Further reading by Brian Cox

- *The Great Betrayal: Memoirs of a Life in Education.* Chapmans. 1992

READING STANDARDS

Arthur De Caux, Senior Assistant Secretary,
National Association of Head Teachers

There is, about some of the statements made on reading standards, a hint of the pre-Maastricht caricature of the Englishman abroad. If you shout 'phonics' loudly enough in all directions, reading ills will be cured and educationists firmly put in their place. Nevertheless, it is right and proper that reading should remain at the top of the educational agenda, if only because it is the only one of the 3 Rs which actually begins with R.

No standards will ever be high enough. What is not right and proper is for detractors to make relentless outbursts which feed banner headlines with criticisms of teachers and teaching methods, when the criticisms are simply not borne out by repeated investigation and enquiry. The result of such activity has been to polarise debate to a dangerous degree. It is dangerous because it prevents institutions, schools and teachers from evaluating calmly and reasonably what they are doing. Any self-criticisms, doubts, questionings or modifications are immediately seized upon as serious admissions of failure, if not a deliberate conspiracy to keep the nation illiterate. The main thrust of the detractor's argument is that there is a single and foolproof method of teaching reading which teachers refuse to use because they have been brainwashed into using an alternative method which does not work. Yet it has been repeatedly demonstrated that teachers use a variety of methods in their efforts to find one or a combination which works best for each child. This may include, where appropriate, the method favoured by the detractors. How have we reached this position of perpetual wrangling, which is unsettling for teachers and, above all, parents?

Since 1991 alone we have had the 'real books' scare in which it was asserted that reading standards had fallen quite markedly because teachers had abandoned any kind of structure or scheme and relied instead on a kind of osmosis taking place when children picked up real books and attempted to read them. The publicity was enough to encourage the then Secretary of State to ask HMI to investigate, and the Schools Examination and Assessment Council (SEAC) to survey evidence of reading standards held by local authorities. At the same time the Education Science & Arts Committee (ES&A) was spurred into an investigation of its own.

The message from all three reports was broadly the same, and summarised in these extracts from the HMI report , 'The Teaching and Learning of Reading in Primary Schools'. In this instance HMI, with exemplary clarity and lack of coded language, say it all. It is illuminating to read the report in full (former DES reference 10/91/NS):

> '76   The effective teaching of reading calls for skills and knowledge to be applied consistently and with sufficient flexibility to ensure that children benefit from the appropriate method at the right time. Successful teachers of reading and the majority of schools used a mix of methods each reinforcing the other as the children's reading developed.

> '77   There is no evidence from the survey, or from HMI's visits to schools over the last year, that the so called 'real books' approach or any other single approach to teaching reading is taking the country by storm. It is important to note, however, that in the minority of schools which were wedded to a single method of teaching reading, including devotees of 'real books' and phonics, failure was more prevalent than in schools using a combination of methods.'

A survey of the members of the National Association of Head Teachers confirmed the findings of these reports. Nevertheless, the attacks on reading standards continued with the focus changing from 'real books' to 'nothing but the phonics'.

Further general misery was spread by the misrepresentation of the 1991 Key Stage One assessment results. First an article appeared in a Sunday newspaper declaring that '28% of seven year olds could not read, could not recognize 3 letters of the alphabet'. The results were published the following Thursday to further headlines of a similar nature and features on all the news programmes. By 'Question Time' on BBC 1 that evening all four panel members accepted it as a fact that 28% of the nation's 7-year-olds could not read. Let us leave for another argument the flawed nature of a first national pilot scheme which produced these results.   The facts behind 'the 28%' are these:

- 2% of pupils were awarded W (working towards level 1)
- 26% were awarded level 1.

The achievement of level 1 requires recognition of individual letters of the alphabet. This means that only 2%, not 28%, could conceivably be regarded as not recognising three letters of the alphabet. More serious is the fact that the pupils who form the 26% at level 1 range from clear non-readers (number unknown) who only just managed to achieve level 1 to others (number unknown) who were very close to level 2 and could not be described as unable to read.

Further, the award of level 2 depended largely on the interpretation by teachers of the statement of attainment, 'read a range of material with some independence, fluency, accuracy and understanding'.

Faced with completely new and virtually unmanageable assessment arrangements, teachers displayed their natural caution and were reluctant to place pupils at level 2 unless they were confident of being able to justify it, especially as these assessments are supposed to be no more than diagnostic. Having seen their caution rewarded by headlines implying that teachers were to blame for a decline in standards, little wonder if they muttered to themselves, 'We won't be caught like that again'.

There has been a further unhelpful development. In the review of the 1991 pilot scheme, many teachers indicated that the level 2 band was too large. The government added in 1992 an A-E scale at level 2 based on a simple word count of just twenty-five words in which seven words could discriminate across all five grades and the difference between 2B and a 2D could be the stumbling (by a 7-year-old) over just three words.

This absurdity could have serious consequences if some people, possibly in high places, suddenly regard a 2D as evidence of failure or inability to read. More to the point is the frustration felt by teachers at the arbitrary imposition of a dotty system which the government now seeks to justify on the grounds that teachers said they wanted it. These events at the very least suggest that fears which are raised repeatedly about standards and methods are largely unfounded and often distorted. This does not mean that there are not genuine concerns about reading standards but they are more to do with wider issues than what goes on in the classroom. The changes in society over the last thirty years have made the teaching of reading much more difficult. The cosy image of well-spoken children, watching only the occasional uplifting television programmes, being read to at every sensible bedtime and coming home from school eager to get to grips with Jane Austen in front of a log fire, the steaming mug of Ovaltine within comfortable reach, is not recognised by many teachers.

The NFER report 'Reading in Recession' published in 1992 treated the matter more seriously. Few would seek to dispute the sources of evidence quoted in that report, which confirm that children's literacy, and in particular their reading attainment, are related to aspects of their home background.

The NFER report goes on to chart the changing patterns of family life and composition, and of employment, resulting in the growth in the number of establishments providing substitute care for children under 5. In short, more time has to be found by hard-pressed teachers or support staff for reading recovery in some form as well as for initial reading itself.

This takes us to the other and more serious area of concern. The intensity and amount of change brought about by the Education Reform Act has considerably reduced the time which initial training institutions and teachers can devote to the teaching of reading skills. Another recent survey by the NFER found that all methods of teaching reading were offered to students, with phonics a component part. Yet many graduates stated they had learned little or nothing about phonics during their course, nor did they feel confident about applying their knowledge in the classroom. The signs are all there that everyone is being asked to do too many things, too cursorily, too quickly.

The same applies to the teachers in the classroom faced with endless attainment targets and programmes of study. At last the DFE and NCC recognise that it is all too much. Meanwhile, it is very possible indeed that reading standards have begun to slide as teachers have been diverted away from their first priority.

How do we go forward in a positive and realistic way? *First,* by taking some comfort from the comment by Professor Asher Cashdan in 'Education' of 18 September 1992:

> *'Many, as has always been the case, largely teach themselves to read, with environmental assistance both in and out of school and helped by a variety of adults as well as the teacher.'*

Parents are vital, not only in what they achieve pre-school in reading with their own children but later in collaboration with the teachers. At the heart of Home School Partnerships usually lie shared activity to promote children's reading.

Second, we go forward by reviewing initial training and National Curriculum requirements to allow trainers and teachers more time, for which there is no substitute, to do their jobs properly. *Third,* by the government taking the lead in promoting the proper climate in which sensible and professional debate of important issues can take place without dogmatic polarisation and repeated setbacks to the morale of all concerned. *Fourth,* by making resources available for reading recovery programmes where objective research shows that standards have fallen (for these purposes whether the fault lies with teaching methods, social upheavals or curriculum overload, it matters not). *Finally*, but of first importance in this matter, by remembering that the child who needs to learn to read is more important than anybody else.

EXAMINATION RESULTS

Michael Duffy, Headteacher of King Edward VI School, Morpeth

Examinations are an enormously important part of the education system of England and Wales. We probably spend more time putting our children through them than any other country, and much more money too. In secondary schools the cost of public examinations, in entry fees alone, is close to £40 a year for each pupil on the roll, very near the average amount that schools spend per pupil on books, equipment and materials. Given those figures, it is perhaps surprising that not many users of the system (and that includes parents and employers and many students too) really understand what those examinations measure.

Or is it so surprising? Until recently, not all schools have been very helpful. Now it is widely recognised that schools owe it to their parents (and certainly to their students) to take them into partnership, as it were, on the complications that arise from such a complex system. Most schools are now much better at that task. Those that are not, the ones that don't explain the grading system, for instance, or the weightings given to different aspects of the syllabus, or the complications of the different entry levels, will soon improve, if parents gently ask the questions.

But even those schools can't take all the blame. The truth is that in this country (and the reasons go back at least a hundred years) we have over-estimated what examinations can do. Until the National Curriculum was introduced, for instance, we used to invent a new examination if we wanted to change what was actually taught in schools. That was why A/S Level was devised. A Levels were seen as too narrow in their subject area: so the solution was to create a new examination that covered half as much ground and encourage students to take one or more of those as well. That was (and is) confusing to the users. Post-16, where the National Curriculum does not apply, new examinations are still seen as the way to change the content of taught courses but they are being added to the existing collection, in the hope that 'the market' (in other words, what parents and employers want) will sort things out.

The government has not helped. It has put an enormous emphasis on examinations. Schools have to publish the results in great detail and in standard form (no harm in that) so that local league tables can be compiled from which parents can find out, we are told, how their school is doing.

Part of the trouble is that league tables of results can't tell you that. To know how a school is doing, you need to know where it started from.

Some schools with a lot of clever children actually do rather badly by them, and some whose children tend to come from unfavourable backgrounds do rather well: but league tables of results won't tell you which. Close enquiry and visits to the school will actually tell you more. Besides which, the results that you are interested in are those that your child will achieve. The points score for the school won't tell you that. The other problem with league tables is that they make the results rather more important than they are. The old School Certificate, and even the O Level that replaced it, were school-leaving examinations. What sort of job you got, or what training opportunity, or what sixth form course, depended on how well you did. That is not the case with GCSE, which serves instead as an indication of what a student has learned so far, and how well she/he has learned it. It shows what sort of training students need, or what sort of further education. It does not close doors. A Level still does, of course: which is one of the reasons why so many influential bodies outside the schools would like to see A Level reformed on the GCSE or Continental model.

I said that GCSE is an indication of a student's learning. That raises another important point. Examining in this country is very skilfully done: the different examining boards have a huge reservoir of experience and expertise to draw upon. But educational examining is an art, not a science. It is not like, for example, deciding whether a child can swim 50 metres or play a sheet of music. It's a matter of judgement: first, in selecting questions that will test a pupil's knowledge of the syllabus, and then in determining how well that pupil's answer rates. Generally speaking, examiners do both things very well; but they would be the first to say that they cannot possibly test every pupil's learning. If we, as adults, think of the skills that we have developed in our work, and then ask ourselves how many of those qualities we could demonstrate in an examination room, we get some understanding of the limitations of the process.

We also quickly see that some of the skills we most value are precisely those we could not possibly demonstrate on paper. The great danger of the league-table approach to examination results, where parents are concerned, is that it will push schools into concentrating all their teaching on the things that crop up in examination questions. That would be a disaster. Apart from anything else, it would make a nonsense of the National Curriculum, which very properly includes many attainment targets that only the teacher in the classroom (and, of course, the parent in the home) can sensibly assess.

30

GCSE as it was first conceived was a genuinely wide examination. Unlike O Level, which had a pre-set failure rate as a proportion of the entry, it laid down broad categories of achievement for the different grade levels, and it looked for practical capability and understanding as well as memorised knowledge. In every subject, internally assessed coursework was required as well as the examination paper, and skilled `moderators' went from school to school to check that assessments were consistent.

These two factors significantly improved performance. All over the country, schools reported that pupils who would otherwise have been written off as failures were responding to the challenge of showing what they knew and could do. That was not unexpected. Sir Keith Joseph, who as Secretary of State had given the go-ahead to GCSE in 1984, had specifically said that he expected it to produce a marked improvement in performance. In the event, that was exactly what happened. Nationwide, the proportion of candidates getting grades A-C rose from below 40% in 1987 (the last O Level year) to 42% in 1988, 46% in 1989, and 48% in 1990. By 1992, the figure was 51%.

As the number of candidates was also increasing, proportional to the age group, the improvement was actually somewhat greater. But by this time, of course, a significant number of people on the fringes of the government, anxious lest standards were being diluted, were crying '*foul*'. This reached a climax in August 1992 when the present Secretary of State gave great publicity to a brief report by a group of soon-to-be-disbanded HMIs that said they had `limited confidence' that standards were being maintained. There was something of an outcry, not least from the parents of this year's candidates who thought their offspring had done well, and now were not so sure.

What, precisely, are such parents to believe?

The first pointer is clear from what is said above. GCSE is not about maintaining `standards', but about indicating how much children know, understand, can do. Examinations do not set standards unless, that is, they set the same questions every year, or fail the same proportion of the intake. The first is obviously absurd, and the second has been tried and found to be extravagantly wasteful of our children's talent.

The second, is that the HMI report (which is available from HMSO) did not make a convincing case for its conclusion. The criticisms it levelled were criticisms that can be levelled at all examinations that depend on subjective judgement, either in question setting or in marking. The School Examination and Assessment Council, set up by the government to ensure consistency and accuracy in examinations, refused to endorse the HMI opinion. So did the examination boards. And so did HMI in Wales, investigating a similar (but less sharply marked) improvement in results.

The third pointer is rather easier to grasp. It is that, since GCSE was instituted, the success rate has been rising at 18 as well. There has been a sharp increase both in the number of students attempting A Level, and in the number achieving passes. The latter figure has risen from 74% (for the last O Level cohort) to 77% in 1990 and 78.5% in 1992. The Secretary of State has said he looks forward to achieving an A Level pass rate, in the year group as a whole, of 50%. It is not at all clear why he regards a 50% pass rate at A Level as an indication of rising standards, and a 50% pass rate at GCSE as evidence of a decline.

Two final pieces of evidence may be considered. The first is that the introduction of GCSE has coincided with a really marked increase in the number of young people choosing to continue their education full time beyond 16 from 40% in 1986, to more than 60% in 1992. Schools report that the GCSE effect is a significant factor in this presumably desirable increase. And the second? That is really quite intriguing. It is that examination results in Scotland, both for Standard grade and Highers, have risen on a similar curve to those in England and Wales. Perhaps it's not the GCSE effect, after all, but simply better teaching, or better parental backing. Individual readers must draw their own conclusions.

The best advice, I think, is to take all broad conclusions from league tables and results with just a pinch of salt. Except, of course, where your own child is concerned. Those are the ones that matter, and the ones that with your school, you can certainly interpret.

THE ELUSIVENESS OF QUALITY

*Duncan Graham, Visiting Professor of Education, Manchester University,
and Former Chairman of the National Curriculum Council*

Educationists have laid forth about standards for generations, but they have been reluctant about measuring them. They have been long on assertion ('the best school in the country/county/town') and short on proof. They were wide open when, in the seventies and eighties, parents, public and industrialists began to worry even more than normal about standards and quality.

The government then found it convenient to express great concern about falling standards, apparently based on distrust of modern teaching methods, and international comparisons which, though difficult to interpret, seemed to confirm that all was not well.

A collective mass hysteria

The result has been a kind of mass hysteria about standards and at times an impression created that we positively want things to be as bad as possible. Even successes such as the improvements in GCSE results are treated with suspicion. It is not uncommon to hear extreme views in high places, such as a household name industrialist who told me that it was a disgrace that 63% of youngsters left school illiterate. He had misread 6.3% or .63% somewhere. Some people want to believe the worst. While standards are certainly not too high, the problem is that they have not been improving consistently and commensurate with the nation's need to avert a peasant economy by the millennium. That will depend upon the National Curriculum continuing to raise expectations, to encourage consistency and to drive for relevance. But unless schools become better at quality assurance and the rest of us better at judging and assessing it, we may well do no more than continue to worry and damage morale. Governments will get away with policies which conceal their own short-term aims and doctrinaire attitudes, and their avoidance of the 'real' cost of quality education.

The difficulties of measuring quality

Measuring quality and improving it are admittedly difficult; this has sometimes served as an excuse for not trying. It is not good enough. We know what we need to assess.

- quality of teaching and what improves it (training)
- adequacy of resources
- management
- quality of assessment mechanisms.

At school level the government White Paper 'Choice and Diversity'(1992) lays down key conditions as:

- a high level of parental and community support
- clear and widely understood objectives
- consistently high expectations of pupils
- thorough monitoring and review of performance.

That seems reasonable as far as it goes, but is short on teaching quality and what parents clearly worry about - class sizes, teachers, provision of books and equipment. For motivation the government relies on 'market forces'. It claims that competitive markets support success; unfortunately they also reinforce failure. A broader range of motivating factors is required involving encouragement, celebration of success, restoration of public confidence, and perhaps above all a measure of 'value added'. This is quite a different thing from examination results.

There is now a clear consensus about the need to put quality at the top of the agenda. Less unanimity exists about how to achieve it. What is deeply worrying is that the traditional sources of quality control are being phased out, and what will replace them seems unlikely to work better, if as well. A quality-control 'black hole' yawns at our feet. Could it be that there are vested interests which do not relish independent judgements and do not appreciate that achieving quality may require external inspection of schools but infinitely more requires continuous review, advice and encouragement, not to mention resources?

What is in place now?

The structure up until now has its imperfections, but is not without merit. We have had for more than a century HMI, an independent body which could advise the Secretary of State as it saw fit, and whose Annual Reports could be, and were, embarrassing to government. With numbers somewhat over 400, HMIs were capable of assessing evidence, exercising judgement, and pronouncing with authority. Their replacement with Ofsted (the Office for Standards in Education), with less than half the number of inspectors, does not inspire confidence, in spite of claims about independence and impartiality. Significantly, a 1992 Annual Report on schools seems unlikely.

HMI have worked increasingly with the Advisers and Inspectors employed by local authorities. Their inspection methods have been brought into line, permitting most schools to be given a regular review and follow-up support.

Snapshot portraits of schools (or of any organisation) have their limitations: it is not unknown for displays to be laid on for the camera! Many LEAs, including Cambridge, Suffolk, Bradford and Birmingham have developed systems which are both sophisticated and rigorous. The pending demise of LEAs will leave a huge gap in support.

The 1988 Education Reform Act set up two new bodies to give independent professional advice to the Secretary of State. Politicians need the help and advice of professionals in education as in all specialist areas. They cannot get it from a generalist corps of civil servants. Clearly they need to weigh advice carefully; 'experts' have to be watched. But they still need to have this advice loud and clear and publicly. The National Curriculum Council and the Schools Examination and Assessment Council (soon to be amalgamated) have seen their membership changed from professional to politically compromised: they seem to say what government wants to hear. A potentially objective voice has become muted. One bright feature is the existence of a national teacher appraisal system, a welcome first for England. In common with the best practice in industry and the services, it is supportive, developmental, and challenging. It will improve standards - provided that it is not hijacked into becoming too crude a part of a merit pay system.

In recent years there has been a welcome involvement of governors and parents in school management and therefore in quality control. Unfortunately it has coincided with the decline of just those bodies which might have been expected to support and advise. The league tables approach has probably done more to open the eyes of governors to the inadequacies of crude statistics than it has to helping them bring about improvements. Left to themselves parents and governors tend to narrow the scope of education when it needs to be broadened. We need the basics (on which the evidence paradoxically is that too much time is spent) but we need so much more to ensure both mature citizens and a well-equipped, well-motivated work-force. Parents know their limitations. Few would agree unreservedly with the Secretary of State that: *'parents know best the needs of their children, certainly better than educational theorists or administrators and better even than our mostly excellent teachers.'*

('Choice and Diversity'. 1992: P. 2 Para. 1.6)

Parents are having greatness thrust upon them. Partnership would be better. Another worrying feature is the plans to inspect schools every four years by teams recruited by Ofsted from the private sector. They will tender for the contracts, and presumably the cheaper the better. In spite of the safeguards, the training of inspectors and the oversight of the new Chief Inspector, it is hard to see how consistency will be achieved, and the back-up which schools need will be provided. Ironically, most of the private sector inspectors will be recruited from those made redundant by HMI and LEAs. Will this be good or bad? Incidentally parents will have to queue up at the local library to see the one copy of the report available to them!

What is required?

What we need is a coherent plan to build on the available resources. There must be clarity about the advantages and limitations of league tables, new-style inspections, market forces, choice and so on. We cannot turn the clock back but both parents and public need to be satisfied that Ofsted will be independent and properly funded, and that the new system will be buttressed by something which adequately replaces LEA support between and after inspections.

The most striking omission from what we have now and what is proposed is direct involvement of schools and teachers. It is all too top-down, too imposed. In business and commerce the government has encouraged self-help and working to gain accreditation. It has supported the BS5750 approach which gives kite marks for quality and accredited proof of excellence. The process is not directly appropriate for schools, although fifteen or so have gone through it, but the procedures are relevant. They guarantee recognition as a result of an organisation's own efforts. It would not be difficult to work up a system whereby a school gains accreditation progressively for management (BS5750 would do); staff training and appraisal (national scheme exists); curriculum organisation and delivery (based on the National Curriculum); and finally assessment.

Schools, properly accredited, should be trusted to do their own National Curriculum assessment, up to age 16 at least: that must be better than the unseemly wrangles over GCSE results. The model exists with the post-16 National Vocational Qualifications. Think what it could all do for morale, and more importantly standards. Parents and governors would be involved and reassured. Employers could trust the 'Kite mark'. With national validation it could restore the credibility so sadly lacking now. It is time for all the partners to unite in ensuring quality instead of resorting to recriminating about it.

Who will take the initiative?

Further reading by Duncan Graham

- *The National Curriculum - a lesson for us all. Routledge.* November 1992.

- *Sense Nonsense and the National Curriculum;* with Michael Barber. Falmer. January 1993.

FACING THE FACTS? HISTORY IN SCHOOLS AND THE NATIONAL CURRICULUM

Chris Husbands, School of Education, University of East Anglia

On 1st October 1992 the Prime Minister's Office released a letter to Fred Jarvis, the former general secretary of the National Union of Teachers. In it Mr Major is reported to have said that there was 'no dispute' that history had been the victim of an insidious attack by progressive educationists who had put too much stress on skills such as analysing the validity of data instead of teaching 'the facts'.

National Curriculum History was introduced from September 1991, after a furious, often ill-tempered and ill-informed debate about what sort of history children should be taught and how they should learn it. Critics of classroom history argued that it rewarded abstract and 'woolly' skills at the expense of a rigorous grounding in historical 'facts'; that 'new' versions of school history concentrated on the experiences of the poor and the dispossessed at the expense of the 'real' history of kings and queens; and that pupils simply did not learn enough dates.

Polarised positions were taken up, and often false distinctions drawn between 'skills' and 'facts', between 'traditional' and 'progressive' history. The Statutory Orders for the National Curriculum steered a sophisticated compromise between the extremes, and offered a framework for history teaching which commanded widespread support among the profession.

In the autumn of 1992, attacks on school history were revived. A fortnight before the Prime Minister's letter, the 'Campaign for Real Education' argued that 'progressive educationists' had taken control of National Curriculum History, which is 'ideologically tainted and makes no sense in the classroom'. The Secretary of State for Education appointed critics of National Curriculum History to the History committee of the Schools Examination and Assessment Council (SEAC). One of them was unsparing in his criticism of National Curriculum History:

'At present, pupils can cover the knowledge required by National Curriculum History in subjects such as the Industrial Revolution or how women won the vote in a morning'. He went on 'It is sad that it has required action from so high a quarter (the Prime Minister) *to raise the question of a review'.*

The debate about history is bedevilled by an assumption that in many ways history should be if not an easy subject then at least a straight-forward one. There is a feeling that its area of concern is the past and learning about it should be a simple matter of acquiring the 'facts'. The reality is rather different. There are three linked questions. The first is to do with *why* we teach history at all in schools; the second with *what* history should be taught, and the third with *how* it should be taught.

Why teach history in schools?

At the root of the debate over school history is an argument about what history in schools is for. The 'Campaign for Real Education' insists that there is one reason only for teaching history - to introduce children to the culture and civilisation of which they are part: '*initiating children into the mysteries of our own civilisation is the main reason for having history on the timetable in state-funded schools*'.

Fifty years ago this version of history as celebration seemed almost justifiable: the world map was largely coloured red, and history could be presented as the account of the rise of an empire upon which the 'sun never set'. But national and global realities have changed. We can no longer be so confident of our place in the world. History is now an account not just of our 'rise' but of our decline too. As our role in the world has changed so accounts of our own past have become more complex. The make-up of our own population has changed. Like it or not - and I personally find it an exciting, stimulating reality - we are a multi-cultural nation. Our cities, our small towns and our villages are culturally diverse. Our children will grow up into a society more polyglot than the one we knew as children. What can history offer to this sort of society?

What it cannot do is simply to celebrate the past. There is no single, easily understood and easily transmitted culture. We live in a country whose language and culture has been shaped and enriched by a series of invasions and migrations. In this nation, understanding that our society is diverse, and has diverse, often competing traditions, is a valuable part of being able to contribute to it as an adult.

What sort of history?

What, then, about the 'facts' and the 'dates'? No one would dispute that gaining knowledge about the past is an important outcome of studying history. We want pupils to build up knowledge of the past. But this is far from straight-forward. There *is* simply too much history for any child to learn it all, and some selection has to be made.

It follows from what has been argued so far that the criteria by which content is selected need to reflect the diversity of the society in which we live: British history, yes, but also the history of other parts of the world, both those closely connected to us by ties of tradition and culture and, importantly, parts of the world distant and remote from this island. It follows too that local history is important; as Sir Keith Joseph once observed, we might teach history differently in St Helens as compared to the way we teach it in Dorset. It follows that history needs to be concerned with kings and queens, but also with the humbler, though no less important experiences of ordinary men and women in past times.

Any version of school history which concentrated on one of these types of history - national history, or high political history, or simply local history would be an inadequate history, selling our children short. But publicly agreed and debated criteria for the selection of historical content are an important guarantee of a quality historical education. The National Curriculum tries to ensure this.

A core of study units guarantees access for children to a range of British (not simply English) historical experience, and, for the first time, teachers need to choose a balanced range of other areas of history which will ensure that all children, for example, study the past of a non-European society. And throughout, the National Curriculum orders insist that teachers introduce children to the diverse experiences of different ethnic groups and men and women in societies in the past.

The facts and the evidence

Some people, of course, would prefer a more directive approach: a list of names and dates which children have to learn. It follows from what has been argued so far that such a list would be undesirable. It is highly unlikely that we could generate a manageable list of names and dates which would command widespread support: some events - some whole historical periods - would be omitted which many people might claim were of fundamental importance. To construct such a list for a National Curriculum would entail decisions about which names and dates were to be taught to primary school children and which to secondary school children. But it is difficult to see how some dates could be described as 'easier' or 'more difficult' than others: at what age, for example, should children learn about the Industrial Revolution? Is it more, or less difficult than the feudal system? Such an approach would be endlessly, pointlessly, complex.

Over and above these technical difficulties about content there are some more fundamental objections to constructing a history curriculum around facts and dates. Knowing about the past is never just about knowing when things happened. If pupils do not know why they happened, what consequences they had and what effects they had, then knowing about history is reduced to a sort of disjointed Mastermind: one specialist subject after another. But learning history simply is not like that. In many cases historians cannot be sure about what actually happened, or why it happened, or what its consequences actually were.

The evidence simply does not exist, or eye-witnesses and others disagree. How much, for example, do we really know about Boudicca? Why was there a Peasants' Revolt in 1381 - was it a spontaneous protest against the poll tax, or a manifestation of deeper tensions in later medieval society? Looked at like this, history is infinitely more complex than a list of dates and facts; it is about developing critical skills in locating, interpreting and evaluating the evidence which is available. It is about asking questions of that evidence.

The intellectual cutting edge of history is precisely provided by the basic idea that we cannot quite be sure that the answers we give to questions about the past are right, but that they seem to be borne out by the evidence. The three attainment targets of National Curriculum History address themselves to these ideas: that learning history depends on using the evidence, on interpreting points of view, on being able to set events in the context of their causes and consequences.

The National Curriculum, though far from perfect, is a professional attempt to define a workable school history which reflects the concerns of teachers, academic historians and parents. It accepts that history is more than a rag-bag of 'good stories' and that 'doing' history is an intellectually reputable pursuit for children and their teachers. It accepts too, often in a tentative and cautious way, that many of the 'answers' to questions we all want to ask about the past - what was it like? how do we know it was like that ? what did people think ? - are not easy to answer. The real tragedy of the current assault on National Curriculum History is that every day, in primary and secondary classrooms throughout the country, teachers and their pupils are engaging with questions like these and demonstrating not just that they are intellectually respectable but that they are realisable in the classroom.

The politically influential far Right offers children and their teachers a version of learning history which is intellectually impoverished and educationally barren, which will drive down teachers' expectations and cramp children's intellectual development.

Why does it all matter?

The Czech dissident author Milan Kundera offered an explanation:

'People are always shouting that they want to create a better future. It's not true. The future is an apathetic void of no interest to anyone. The past is full of eager life, there to irritate us, provoke and insult us, tempt us to destroy it or repaint it. The only reason people want to be masters of the future is to change the past. They are fighting for access to the laboratories where photographs are retouched and biographies and history re-written'.

16-19 EDUCATION

Louise Kidd, Principal of Rutland Sixth Form College
and President of the Secondary Heads Association

Introduction

During the 1980s both the government and the CBI identified that the participation rate in post-compulsory education in Britain was below that of other industrialised nations. In recent years great strides have been made to rectify this situation and these achievements should be a source of pride for all concerned; government, educators and students.

It is bewildering, therefore, to witness the persistent attacks on education which seek not to praise but to undermine and belittle this success.

The CBI set ambitious targets in 1989 which were accepted as national targets by all political parties. These targets, summarised below, set goals not only for full-time participation rates but also for levels of achievement at 18 and increased uptake in higher education.

- By 1997 80% of young people to attain NVQ level II or its academic equivalent (five GCSEs at grades A-C).

- All young people to be entitled to structured training, work experience or education leading to NVQ level III or its academic equivalent.

- By the year 2000 50% of the age group should attain NVQ level III or its academic equivalent.

- Education and training provision should be structured and designed to develop self-reliance, flexibility and broad competence as well as specific skills.

(adapted from *Towards a Skills Revolution.* CBI)

I believe that schools and colleges have reacted positively to national priorities and there have been marked improvements in all the areas of post-compulsory education identified by national bodies. I believe that praise and congratulation for these not insignificant improvements must go to teachers, as well as institution's managers who, with some funding help from the Training, Enterprise and Education Directorate (TEED) of the Employment Department, have planned and revised aspects of quality within their institutions.

I will endeavour to outline the positive achievements in 16-19 education under the following major headings:

1. Participation rates post-16 and the Advanced Level examination

2. BTEC provision

3. Post-16 initiatives

4. Participation in higher education

1. Participation rates

Participation rates in full-time education have continually increased since 1974, with a particularly rapid increase from 1987 onwards. In 1990 the participation rate in full-time education was 37% compared to 33% in 1986. However, since 1990 when the first GCSE cohort gained their qualifications, the participation rate has in reased by a dramatic 2-3% per year, signifying without doubt that examination success leads to significant improvements in willingness to continue in education, especially in the cohort who achieve modest success (GCSE grades D-G).

Furthermore, although there has been an increase in the uptake of the A Level examination since 1987 which corresponded with the rapid increase in post-compulsory education in that year, the standards achieved at Advanced Level have continued to rise. The rise from 1990 corresponds also with the first GCSE cohort taking Advanced Level examinations.

Advanced Level results

Year	% Grades A-C	% Passes	Number of candidates
1989	43.0	75.7	642,977
1990	43.7	76.7	657,421
1991	44.2	77.8	695,991
1992	46.4	79.6	730,212

I believe these results reflect a good learning environment in schools and colleges, promoted by a dedicated teaching force. These factors and achievements at GCSE have increased students' motivation and will to achieve.

HMI in their annual reports have confirmed the quality of teaching at A Level when they have consistently reported, since 1990, that over 80% of all A Level lessons have been of sound quality.

2. BTEC provision

One of the alternatives to A Level that is becoming inceasingly popular is BTEC. The BTEC First Diploma is targeted at students with modest GCSE results who would normally have entered the job market at 16. It has also proved a real alternative to repeating GCSE qualifications in year 11 with around 60% of students remaining in full-time education for a further two years.

First-year registrations for BTEC programmes for the 1991/92 academic year have topped 277,000, an increase of 12% over the 1990/91 figure and a growth of 55% in a five-year period. Furthermore, the trend towards full-time education is reflected in a 48% drop in both First and National Certificate programmes, which are usually part-time, with a corresponding increase in the full-time Diplomas of 48% for the First and 21% for the National. This increase has no doubt partially been due to the ability of schools to offer the First Diploma since 1991 when around 300 courses were approved. By September 1992 the number of accredited courses in the school sector had doubled to 600. This increase in BTEC provision has taken place simultaneously with the increase in A Level uptake against a background of falling numbers reaching the school-leaving age.

These statistics, I believe, clearly reflect the strategic planning of schools and colleges to provide a variety of suitable courses for the increased student population which is now spread over a much wider ability range. In addition, BTEC courses have proved a valuable base for students to progress up the qualifications ladder.

The BTEC National Diploma has also shown that it is a real alternative to Advanced Level for many students. In 1989, 46% of students with BTEC National qualification gained employment, whilst 50% went on to higher education, with less than 3% not in employment or higher education. The BTEC completion rate of over 90% after one year for its First Diplomas and 80% after two years for its National qualifications is indeed an enviable record of success.

3. Post-16 initiatives

Funding from the Department of Employment, particularly through the Technical and Vocational Education Initiative (TVEI), has been and still is promoting a climate which I believe is improving the quality of education experience available to our young people. TVEI itself has directly spanned a wide range of developments from Education Business Partnership to Flexible Learning Initiatives, from the Recording of Achievement to supporting Individual Action Planning. At the same time a number of separate initiatives have thrived in this climate.

(i)   The University of Cambridge module bank system, which allows students to achieve Advanced Supplementary and Advanced Level qualifications by successfully completing a required number of modules over a five-year period. The modular approach allows students to aim for short-term goals and accumulate credits over a period of time, thus giving students more choice and control over what they study.

(ii) The Wessex project which provides scope through a core and module arrangement to broaden the base of Advanced Levels by placing increased emphasis on skill acquisition to complement knowledge and understanding gained through study.

(iii) A Level enhancement projects, which are based on student entitlement in terms of skills and competencies delivered through a variety of teaching methodologies and learning contexts designed to enhance the opportunities and experiences of students within subject areas.

(iv) The increase in general studies programmes in schools and colleges to promote the TVEI aims of breadth and balance in student programmes.

The processes and initiatives outlined above have enhanced the quality of experiences available to young people in post-compulsory education today.

4. Participation in higher education

As the number of students continuing in education at 16+ has increased along with their performance in examinations at 18+, it is not surprising that there has also been a rise in the number of students entering higher education. The statistics below show that the calibre of candidates based on A Level points scores entering university has not changed significantly despite a rapid expanision in university entrance.

Year	Mean A Level points scores	Number of candidates accepted
1989	21.9	87,013
1990	21.2	99,377
1991	21.1	106,717

(adapted from *UCCA statistical supplements.*)

However, what I believe to be more significant is the increase of women attending university in a full-time and part-time capacity. For example, the following statistics show the percentage increase in the numbers of men and women attending university since 1970/71:

		University		Polytechnics & colleges		Open University	
		Men	Women	Men	Women	Men	Women
Percentage rise between 1970/71 and 1989/90	Full-time	+20	+122	+59	+48	-	-
	Part-time	+72	+283	+45	+758	+236	+740

(adapted from *Education Statistics for the United Kingdom.* HMSO)

Conclusions

I believe that since the introduction of GCSE teachers in schools and colleges as well as the new examinations have successfully raised awareness amongst young people of the value of continuing in full-time education beyond compulsory schooling. This has resulted not only in increased participation but also in higher expectations of young people to continue in education beyond 18. The statistics presented demonstrate that standards of achievement have risen at 18, that students are seeking alternative pathways at 16, that institutions are providing them, and that success in these routes is also being achieved. Furthermore, in a time of diminishing resources, schools and colleges are developing a range of courses to broaden the educational experience of the young people of today, the adults of tomorrow.

I believe students, teachers and managers deserve congratulation. They have increased participation and have raised standards. Teachers have improved the quality of educational experience of our young people. However, this success should not lead to complacency. Much still needs to be done. With co-operation and dialogue schools and colleges can continue to raise both participation levels and standards of achievement.

urther reading by Louise Kidd

- *The Way Forward.* SHA. 1991
- *Towards a Coherent System.* SHA. 1992.
- *Changes in Education and Training.* (Contribution). David Fulton Publishers. 1992

STANDARDS AND QUALITY
Chris Lowe, Head of Prince William School, Oundle, and
Past President of the Secondary Heads Association

Parents must be confused by the claims and counter-claims made about 'standards' in British schools and the quality of education provided. At one moment they are faced with headlines such as 'Britain's Failing Schools' following the results of a reading survey: the next, they are treated to rave reviews of pupils' GCSE performance.

Sir Claus Moser, in his presidential address to the British Association in 1990, expressed concern over the quality of education received by many young people, and Sir Christopher Ball, in his 1991 Royal Society of Arts report 'Learning Pays', pointed to disillusion amongst post-GCSE pupils at the opportunities offered (or not offered) to them. On the other hand, the examination results at 16+ and 18+ have improved steadily over the past twelve years, and schools have rightly trumpeted them. These various perceptions may appear to be contradictory but in fact they only emphasise different aspects of the same scene; the one celebrates success, the other laments the amount of under-achievement in the system. This dilemma goes to show just how difficult it is to grasp in any satisfactory way the notions of 'standards' and 'quality'.

One of our difficulties is that 'standards' and 'quality' are concepts used indiscriminately and often interchangeably by both politicians and commentators. In the recent White Paper 'Choice and Diversity', we learn that the government is 'firmly wedded to quality within the framework of the National Curriculum, measured by assessment' (para 1.13). In para. 1.21 this becomes 'high standards' that will be 'fostered by testing'. This ingenuous switching between the two words would not matter if it was universally understood. But too often it has resulted in a disservice to schools.

This happened in September 1992 when, following record GCSE results much lauded by ministers, a report by HMI, entitled 'GCSE Examinations: Quality and Standards' was sent to the Secretary of State. HMI's criticisms of the inconsistency of the examination board's grading procedures which, as the report says, 'are neither new nor easy to solve', were taken by the media to put into doubt the whole of the recent GCSE results, a view reinforced by the Secretary of State's immediate public reaction in ordering an enquiry, before the report had been published.

Standards in examinations

This eagerness to equate 'standards' solely with examination results is commonplace, but even in this familiar context the use of the word can be misleading. For example, it might be supposed that 'standards' would be a term applied only to targets which have been set, which can be attained by a particular target group, and which can be measured. Throughout examination history, however, setting such standards has proved an inexact science. The holy grail 'standard' is not somewhere out there waiting to be found. Standards of attainment are set by experienced teacher-examiners, using historical knowledge and personal experience. Their job is made more difficult by having to move from norm-referenced modes, where levels are artificially set, based on previous years' results, to criteria-referencing, where a grade is awarded if a stated target is met. At the moment two systems operate - mainly criteria-referencing for Key Stages One to Three, and mainly norm-referencing for Key Stage Four GCSE assessment.

This has given rise to suspicion about the steep rise in C+ passes, particularly Grade A, since the introduction of GCSE, a suspicion based on the premise that overall levels of performance should remain roughly static. In my own school we were as puzzled as anyone else by the boost in gradings achieved by the first cohort of GCSE candidates. It is now obvious to us that the new, more varied, type of testing and the expansion of the skills being tested allowed far more students to excel than did the narrow scope of the preceding GCE. Once teachers had grown accustomed to the nature of the examination, and more confident about their teaching of the courses it was no longer surprising that student achievement rose. To put their success down to a lowering of standards impugns examiners' integrity and implies a vast conspiracy between hundreds of examiners - not only at GCSE Level, but A Level and degree level, too, since at all these levels student achievement has risen markedly over the past ten years. The Senior Chief HMI reported in 1991 that 'there is no evidence to support the claim that standards in schools are going down'.

Standards, then, indicate the outcomes of the educational process. The 'quality' of education provided is a broader concept which includes 'standards' amongst other factors.

What comprises a 'quality education'?

The quest for higher quality, emphasised in the 1992 White Paper, 'Choice and Diversity', comprises, according to the Secretary of State, 'a national curriculum, greater choice, and accountability, more autonomy and proposals for frequent inspection.' This is not a definition of quality, however; it simply sets out the conditions which, the Secretary of State hopes, will foster high-quality education. All through the document 'quality' is confidently expected to follow from rigorous testing of pupils, assessment of teachers, inspection of schools, and league tables of results. This is the 'stick' approach, consistent with the view that teachers and schools competing against each other will automatically improve standards.

It is a simplistic notion of how good schools operate. It ignores that complex web of interests - pupils', teachers', parents' and governors' - that make up a thriving school community. A high quality of education will depend on all or most of the following - sufficient resources, good facilities, well-trained and well-paid staff, supportive parents and governors, extra-curricular activities, attractive environment, good staff/pupil relationships, pupils' participation in the life of the school, strong leadership. These conditions and inputs are the carrots that lead to high quality.

High quality

The 'quality' of education is, therefore, an amalgam of everything experienced by a child as he or she passes through the school. And in the wake of the many brickbats hurled at youngsters these days it needs to be stated firmly that despite the physical condition of some schools and the inadequate resourcing of most, we have in general a high quality of pupils in our schools, some of the best we have ever had. The work they do in many subjects is well beyond anything that most of their parents had to cope with at school - the National Curriculum ensures that. They often grapple with concepts and skills that were degree level in the 1960s. The majority are as keen to learn as their predecessors. The depth and breadth of their music making, art and design, dance and drama, information technology know-how surpass previous generations, and at the same time, as a generation, they have more concern for those less fortunate than themselves, give more to charity, and show more concern for the environment and for peace in the world. These are manifestations of high-quality education. It is up to parents to see that they are nurtured and acclaimed rather more than mere changes to the system.

Further reading by Chris Lowe

- *School Governors Legal Guide.* Croner
- *The School Governor's Manual.* (Editor). Croner.

THE USES OF COURSEWORK

Michael Marland, Headteacher, North Westminster Community School

Unfortunately, 'coursework' is a vague and ill-defined term that easily attracts criticism. However, anyone really concerned with improving standards in schools would certainly not push proper coursework assignments to one side: far from it. The well-set and well-researched piece of coursework is one of the highest academic achievements of the British secondary school.

Adults have always agonised over how to assess young people's achievements. Changes have been urged on us in the past to make the assessing fairer, more objective, and less likely to be influenced by the background of the pupils. These changes have then been pushed to one side and criticised as 'limited' and 'mechanical'. We introduced the 'eleven plus' examination in the interests of equity and abolished it two decades later for the same reason. We introduced CSE to provide an alternative to O Level, but then had to combine the two for fairness.

When we ended the 'School Certificate' in the early fifties, we raised the key pass threshold, but lowered it again with GCSE. Throughout all those changes we have never properly studied the different assessment methods.

Paul Black's 'TGAT' report was the first government-commissioned study of modes of assessment, but work on the methodology of public examinations has continued to be limited. Earlier, Roger Murphy had shown that multiple-choice questions favoured boys over girls, whereas essay questions did the reverse. There has been some acute research on aspects of assessment, but there has been remarkably little consideration of how the different methods should be used. In all the arguments about how to assess GCSE, there has been nothing said recently about the effect of age. Yet a national study showed that there is a greater likelihood of pupils who are older in the year doing better than those who are younger. Not surprisingly, GCSE (and no doubt its predecessors) have always been what could be called 'ageist'.

'Coursework' is one of those typically vague terms about which people argue because no one knows exactly what it means. What is 'coursework', and why was it developed as a mode of assessing students?

The trouble is that the label can mean many different things:

- at one extreme, the course teacher assesses the standard homework and classwork assignments carried out as part of the course

- sometimes there are specially set pieces of work, which are submitted for the qualification

- often an oral component is included, and the candidate has to demonstrate her or his understanding through exposition or discussion

- for some English courses, a collection of writing of defined categories has to be put together and submitted

- occasionally, as in some history examinations and one Board's 'Science, Technology, and Society', there has to be a major research study, not unlike the thesis of higher degrees.

The Schools Council in the 1970s tried to define the term, but agreement could not be reached. The assessment of pieces of work carried out by the candidate in proper research study conditions, in the candidate's own time, and with the opportunity for reflection and consideration, is neither odd nor sloppy. Indeed, it brings the setting of assignments and the assessing of them nearer to the tasks of the professional, university and business worlds. Time is always at a premium, but what scholarly tasks in any walk of adult life have to be carried out against the clock and with no research tools or opportunity for revision? Politicians deliver their speeches against time, but they prepare them in their own homes at their own speed.

Those who seek rigorous standards in assessment would be well advised to consider 'coursework' as an important tool to balance a fixed time, examination hall, written test. What are the differences? A written examination uses time as the main criteria; the candidate has to write in a sealed hall, with no reference works or notes, against only one challenge, the clock. This tests skills of short-term memory, rapid establishment of what is required, and speedy drafting of a response. It favours boys over girls and the slick over the thoughtful: there is no time for deeper consideration.

In the 1970s research was proposed to establish whether time constraints were more reliable in assessment than other constraints such as length. What would happen to assessment if students had their own choice of time, but had a specified length against which they had to struggle? That is a real intellectual task, pitting research skills against the scope to expand in words.

Journalists would recognise that test, as would lecturers, authors, and other specialists who have to sell their ideas. The Schools Council did not manage to complete that research. It would probably have established that the traditional test against the clock is a less reliable method of assessment than a test against length.

Examination Boards, schools and subject associations began introducing tests other than examinations to provide greater challenge to the student, not to give an easy ride.

It was soon found that setting tasks early in the course so that the student could work at them over a period of time encouraged hard work and pride in that work. The ability of the candidate to define some of the subject tasks in negotiation with the teacher (again as in higher degrees) gave further encouragement and led to deeper thought. The student did not have merely to guess what was in the examiner's mind behind the wording of a terse question: he or she had to probe deeply into the subject matter to devise a focus and a title. Up and down the country, many students were finding an increased challenge and immense pride in the planning and writing up of a range of studies. They were developing information handling skills of a high order that would stand them in good stead in Advanced Level examinations, and higher education. Conversely, some were falling by the wayside as the challenge of such sustained effort was too great for them. This was no soft option.

It is odd that a government that is broadly in favour of making education more 'realistic' is stressing only beating the clock in an examination hall without the normal reference tools of the scholar or writer. Why should a GCSE student be tested only against his or her memory and time skills? At a time when we are all agreed that education should have a greater realism and academic work should be related more closely to vocational activities, the testing of these assignments, which are nearer to real life, should surely be valued.

It is true that there have been difficulties with some 'coursework'. It is sometimes possible that assignments that are outside the scope of the syllabus or incomparable with other assignments could be presented. Comparability is certainly difficult. Indeed, when a student's presentation is judged inadequate the fault may have lain with the teacher agreeing the brief, not the student carrying it out.

There is a fear that work done at home may, at the least, benefit from middle-class book collections and at the worst be deceitful copies of parents' or friends' work. Proper moderation by a team of teachers that includes outside representatives can remove this fear. Other comparability worries are true of all real-life assignments. In fact, it is also true of the unseen examination raced against the clock.

As the 1992 report on GCSE by Her Majesty's Inspectors reminded us, there have always been difficulties in ensuring comparability: assessment of written answers in examinations has its difficulties also. Certainly investment into even further improved moderation would be worthwhile: coursework can be as rigorously assessed as examination papers.

On the other hand, some tasks have been impressively testing. The 'Science, Technology, and Society' examination of the Northern Examining Board has required a research study of some 4,000 words on a topic agreed between student and teacher. The weak candidates have failed to define a problem, seek sources of data and argument, select and judge them, organise the findings, and present the results. Not surprisingly, as this is virtually an undergraduate activity, there is good work mixed with depressing failure. Many have produced startlingly impressive research reports, with cogent arguments, detailed references and lucid text. This is not a lowering of standards, but rather the demanding of intellectual depth.

The Schools Council, which was responsible for curriculum leadership and examination control for twenty years until the late eighties, did not manage to define the most appropriate modes of shaping coursework. However, at its best, there is no doubt that the assessment of a student's skills, knowledge and conceptual understanding can be both more rigorous and more appropriate by the examiners' scrutiny of a research study as part of 'coursework' than an old-fashioned 'stand and deliver against the clock' examination. These answers are often weak, unscholarly and sloppy, whereas the planned and researched longer coursework assignment is often both more practical and more intellectually successful.

There has been very strong evidence from teachers, parents, and students throughout the country that the setting of special coursework assignments and the use of them for assessing the final grade has motivated students very strongly over long periods of time and has improved the quality of the learning achieved. The learning becomes part of the whole course, not merely a preparation for the examination. Motivation and increased understanding thus go together.

We award the highest academic award, the Doctorate of Philosophy, to the postgraduate student who can define a focus of original study, find a range of relevant data and argument, judge the appropriateness of that, organise it, and present it. This is a piece of 'coursework' glorified by the title of a thesis. We do not doubt the validity or reliability of the assessment because the student has offered 'coursework'. This is the pinnacle of study. If this method of assessing achievement is accepted for the highest degrees, why is it so difficult to use it for 16-year-olds? The techniques of controlling the assessment could be further improved by research and development, but the centre of the concept remains sound: the presenting by the candidate of real assignments to be assessed is better teaching, better assessing, and better learning.

Futher reading by Michael Marland

- *The Tutor and the Tutor Group.* Longman. 1989.
- *The Longman Tutorial Resources.* (Six Books). 1989/90.
- *Marketing the School.* Heinemann. 1991.

TEACHING AND LEARNING:
WHAT A CHILD EXPECTS FROM A GOOD TEACHER

Dominic Milroy, OSB, Headmaster of Ampleforth College and
Chairman of the Headmasters' Conference

Parents and teachers

'What did you do at school today?' Every day, millions of parents put this
question to their children, and attach (rightly) the greatest importance to the
answer. They know that, for the child, the encounter with *the teacher* is the
first major step into outside society, the beginning of a long journey towards
adulthood, in which the role of the teacher is going to be decisive. At first, it
is *one* teacher, who represents for the child the world outside home, its
mysterious knowledge, its fascinating skills, its uncharted encounter with
other children. Gradually, the one teacher gives way to many, and the child
begins to perceive that the world of learning is complex and multiple, and
that different teachers represent different areas of skill and knowledge. The
child is naturally disposed to take it for granted that grown-ups *know*
important things and can therefore *teach* them: Uncle Jack's mastery of
football or fly-fishing is as important and as interesting as Miss Jones's
mastery of writing or drawing. But the child has an instinctive respect for the
priority of what is learned at school. Home and school are perceived as the
twin gateways that lead to the grown-ups' world.

The teacher as a professional

The child instinctively expects the teacher to be *professional*. The world of
books and desks and uniforms is a world that speaks of growth and
knowledge. It is a world which is specifically distinct from the world of
home, and which creates its own specific expectations. The child does not
muddle the roles of parent and teacher. It is a pity that in this respect,
grown-ups (represented by government and the media) are often less wise
than the child. The present government's proposals for education (as
represented by the White Paper, July 1992) suggest that parents 'know the
needs of their children... better than teachers' (1.6). This assumption would
be rejected by most wise parents and by all wise children. The natural
expertise of parents lies in one direction, the professional expertise of
teachers in another. The secret of a good school lies in the mutual respect
between parents and teachers: all education is an exercise in *collaborative
parenthood*, in which the *profession* of teaching is seen as a complement to
the *vocation* of parenthood.

The teacher under-valued

In most healthy societies, this complementarity has always been taken for granted, and teaching has been, therefore, perceived as one of the noblest professions, alongside those associated with healing, or citizenship, or caring for the infirm, or creating things of beauty and usefulness. One must ask, at a deep level, why the profession of teaching is so often under-valued in our own society, and to what extend our so-called 'crisis' in education and in society is attributable to an endemic lack of sensitivity to the enormous centrality of the role of teachers. To under-value teachers is to under-value children.

The integrity of the teaching profession

What exactly are we saying when we affirm that the child's instinct is to perceive the teacher as a professional? After all, the majority of teachers down the ages have belonged to no professional association and have had no specific qualifications to teach. They have, rather, been perceived as masters of a specific 'discipline' or body of knowledge, and their authority to teach has been a by-product of this perception. It is an accident of history that the word 'master' has been attached to teaching, and the word 'doctor' to medicine. It is, similarly, a local accident of history that the word 'professor' has, in our own culture, become confined to university teaching. In other European cultures, the three terms are almost interchangeable, and carry equal weight as dignified affirmations of a specific role in society. The teaching profession is, like other professions, an honourable by-product of the existence of institutions of learning, and of a long tradition of professional apprenticeship. This tradition of accredited professionalism is readily accepted in practical fields like medicine, law and accountancy, but teachers have been less fortunate, partly because rapid expansion of population has led to an increased demand for teachers, and to the consequent invention of qualifications which can be seen as devaluing the 'currency' of the teaching profession.

However, the fact remains that the entire educational system, and the network of schools which embodies it, is sustained by a specific professional tradition rooted in the mastery of diverse academic disciplines, and in the skills by which they are communicated. This implies and demands a high level of dedication and of professionalism, and represents a body of experience which exists nowhere else. This experience is concerned above all with meeting the needs and aspirations of countless individual children.

The 'entitlement' of the child

One of the most important aspects of the National Curriculum is the insistence on the entitlement of the child. This means, primarily, that any child who goes to school has the right to encounter a particular and well-defined range of areas of knowledge and skill and to achieve in them a degree of competence appropriate to his or her ability. It is the professional duty of schools and teachers to make sure that this happens. There is, however, a deeper level of entitlement which is harder to define. This is the child's right to real quality of learning. The innate curiosity of children should not be limited by the minimalist requirements of any official curriculum. Nor should it be confined to what is considered to be sociologically useful: children are not simply fodder for the nation's work-force, even though they have the right to be equipped to be members of it. Teachers are, therefore, not in the first instance agents either of the National Curriculum Council (or whatever follows it) or of the State. They are bridges between individual children and the culture to which they belong.

The teacher as a bridge to a wider culture

Children, left to themselves, can easily remain trapped by the concerns and attractions of the immediate present. The role of teachers is to attract them progressively into the many realms of the culture to which they belong. This culture consists partly of a heritage, which links them to the past, and partly of a range of skills and opportunities, which links them to the future.

The role of the teacher is, in this respect, irreplaceable. It may be possible for adults to educate themselves by 'distance learning', with the aid of modern technology, but for children there can be no substitute for the creative relationship with teachers. The role of the teacher is not only to instruct, but also to inspire: the child does not perceive learning as a disembodied pursuit, but as a participation in what the teacher knows. It is this that constitutes the heart of the teaching profession: everything else is rooted in the relationship, at once personal and professional, between the individual teacher and the individual child.

The learning experience

Children long to learn, even if they often show considerable reluctance to face the difficulties which learning implies. They expect the teacher both to recognise the longing and to help them through the difficulties. The learning process, so often taken for granted, is central to education, and is difficult to describe because it varies according to the temperament and ability of each child.

Children do not simply acquire information and skills on a steady, upward curve. They pass, often bumpily, through 'thresholds' of difficulty and of discovery. They learn that new levels of understanding can only be reached by increased levels of patience and concentration. They learn to ask questions of increasing complexity, and to be sceptical of easy answers. They become increasingly aware of the temperamental limitations which inhibit progress, and of the deep links which exist between good learning and good behaviour.

Good teaching

The teacher's contribution to a child's experience of learning has an importance which should be self-evident. There is a tendency nowadays to suggest that a teacher's 'performance' can be readily assessed in terms of 'productivity'. This would be possible only if children arrived at school as uniform bits of raw material capable of being transformed into uniform 'products'. In fact, each child is a mysterious and unique being, often deeply wounded by circumstance, whose true potential may not be realised except in an indefinite future. The teacher is not a manufacturer, but a gardener in an often difficult climate. It is this that makes the teaching profession at once so frustrating, so rewarding and so unquantifiable. The complementarity with parenthood is, again, very clear. The responsibility of the teacher (and of the school) does not stop at the door of the classroom. Every good teacher willingly accepts responsibility for every aspect of a child's arduous journey towards a balanced adulthood, in which moral goodness and civic responsibility are just as important as learning.

The teacher and educational change

It is no doubt the case that bad and ill-directed teaching has been responsible for unacceptably low standards in some of our schools, just as the irresponsible and lax exercise of parental responsibility has led often to unacceptably low standards of social behaviour (as well as complicating the job of teachers). The fact remains, however, that the professional achievement of teachers continues to be huge, and that there is no professional body which knows, collectively, more about education than teachers do. This should not be surprising. What is surprising is that teachers have been asked to play so small a role in current educational reforms. As a result, many avoidable mistakes have been made by legislators, many reforms have been introduced too quickly, and the job of schools and of teachers has become progressively enmeshed by bureaucratic procedures which can only militate against good teaching.

Educational reforms should be binding government and teachers together in a creative partnership. Too often, the reverse is the case. The reform of education is far too important to be coloured either by party politics or by easy media headlines. Somehow, somewhere, the underlying issue of the long-term role of the teacher in our society is not being grasped. The consequences could be very serious.

Further reading by Dominic Milroy

- *Managing Director or Good Shepherd?* Article in *SHA Headlines.*
- *The School's Philosophy* - Chapter for forthcoming book *Head to Head.* John Catt Educational Ltd.

THE CBI VIEW: PUTTING INDIVIDUALS FIRST

Margaret Murray, Head of The Education Policy Group, CBI

The controversy about GCSE begs the question, what are qualifications for? The three groups most entitled to answer that question are students, parents and employers. No one is more keen than employers to see standards rise.

The challenges

The employers' perspective is shaped by the scale of the economic challenge. The accelerating pace of technological advance means that the shelf life of a product can now be as short as three months. With Japan, for example, able to produce and deliver a Nissan car with specific individual touches and extras within 48 hours, business survival depends on maximum flexibility. Employers' expectations of their employees are changing as rapidly as the nature of work itself. They now want employees who are committed to the achievement of corporate objectives - who will use to the full their abilities, ideas and skills.

The contribution of each individual is crucial to the drive for productivity, efficiency, quality and service. Each individual needs to expect change and thrive on it. Our prosperity no longer lies in our hands, but in our brain power. What will give our businesses the edge is the capacity to innovate. The successful organisations of the twenty-first century will be those where all employees are continually learning new skills and adapting their knowledge in order to further the aims of the business.

The skills gap

Employment forecasts are sobering. One estimate predicts that by the year 2000, 70% of all jobs in Europe will require people of professional skills; that is those with A Levels or equivalent and above. Only 30% of jobs will require skills at a level below that, and jobs just requiring manual skills will have almost disappeared. That 70:30 ratio is, broadly, a reversal of the post-war ratio for employment, when about 30% of jobs required professional skills. Yet it is the 30:70 ratio that became institutionalised in our education system. It has excelled in ensuring that about 30% of young people are well qualified. Until recently it has failed the remaining 70%, many of whom have under-achieved. But people are now the key to our competitiveness and we can no longer afford under-achievement. This is where GCSE has a crucial role to play.

·Given the massive gap between where we need to be and where we are, nostalgia for the so-called standards of the past is wasted energy. The standards of our competitor countries are the relevant ones. South Korea aims to have about 80% of its 18-year-old population at higher education entrance standard by the year 2000. The UK's current projection is 33%. In a typical electronics factory in Taiwan, the minimum level of qualification is our equivalent of eight GCSEs at grades A-C. Rather than brood on falling standards, we should concentrate on improving them.

The CBI believes we need nothing short of a skills revolution if the UK is to remain competitive. This means two things: putting individuals first, so that they are helped and motivated to make the maximum use of their talents; and promoting lifetime learning, so that it becomes as essential to our survival as eating and drinking. A root-and-branch attack on our culture of low expectations is long overdue.

Relevant qualifications

Employers want qualifications which empower individuals and raise their aspirations. Such a system should:

1) *Give individuals every chance to achieve, while still being challenged.* One person's success must not be another's failure. A qualification system like the marathon which stretches, differentiates, and enables each to achieve, meets employers' needs far better than the Olympic sprints which are only for a very small elite.

2) *Focus on outcomes or competence making clear what people actually learn, and can do.* National Vocational Qualifications aim to do this and academic qualifications would be enhanced if they were equally explicit.

3) *Develop core, transferable skills,* such as communication, problem solving and personal skills. These are the essential skills which enable individuals to flourish in employment and continue learning, as well as to manage their lives.

4) *Ensure breadth of knowledge and understanding as well as an awareness of their limitations.* High flyers are most aware of what they do not know.

5) *Enable breadth of opportunity, and progression.* Qualifications should open more doors rather than close them.

The GCSE, though not perfect, fares distinctly better than O Levels against these criteria. It should be strengthened once the National Curriculum is fully in place, and, for the first time, the national standards are known and understood by all. GCSE coursework also has a fundamental role to play in raising standards, as long as it is rigorously assessed. Cheating must not be possible. Employers want to be confident that qualifications are an accurate reflection of the individual's ability.

Where coursework is rigorously assessed, it is particularly beneficial in developing core skills, and preparing young people for the realities of working life. A Levels, of course, do not fully satisfy these criteria. The system of A Levels has served us well in the past but it needs to be enhanced if it is to contribute to meeting the pressures not only of the future but also those of today. The need for coherence and breadth in all 16-19 qualifications remains a major objective of CBI education policy.

Employers have been just as unambitious as educators in their expectation of what individuals can achieve when they work in an environment which allows them maximum scope. We have some outstanding examples of what can be done but they are few and far between. They must become the norm. The National Education and Training Targets provide a focus. The task is challenging, and there is substantial resistance. The alternative is to *do what we have always done.* We will then *get what we have always got.* If we are genuinely interested in economic prosperity and effective public services, that is an option we should reject.

WHAT DOES IT ALL MEAN?

Joan Sallis, President of The Campaign for State Education

The clamour of politicians and tabloids for a return to some half-remembered golden age bewilders parents. It's not surprising that they repeat like demented parrots, when approached by an earnest face above a clipboard, that education has gone to the dogs. But when asked about the school their child attends a majority reply that it's a purposeful place; that the children love going there and get on well; that the teachers are hardworking and really care; and that the range of things children learn is astonishing. No, perhaps their spelling and tables don't compare with our day. But they do know what proportion of the world is Chinese and why there were as many grooms and blacksmiths in their town in the census of a hundred years ago as there are motor mechanics now. Meanwhile, a 7 year-old sets the video for his granny.

This shows that the debate about standards passes most parents by. They just don't know what standards are and how they are measured. There are, however, a few things they are very sure about. One is that education is vital, not just to survival in the hard world of work but also for a life of meaning and fulfilment. Secondly, that we spend too much time on measuring and testing and not enough money on what is found to be deficient: you don't make things heavier by weighing or longer by measuring. Thirdly, that childhood cannot be repeated and that life offers few second chances.

Buried here are many clues to what this captive audience might think about the play if only the critics would stop drowning it in abuse. We shall come to these thoughts later. For now it's also important to say that if parents ever do criticise the real schools they know about, it's that the schools make them feel inadequate and unconfident; make them afraid their question is trivial; do not explain things clearly in simple language; and do not want to hear what they think, not really.

Our schools still suffer the backlash against the excesses of the late fifties and sixties. Most reforms overshoot their target and have to be dragged back, and unfortunately are often dragged too far. We suffered from the unavoidable but indecent haste with which the system was rebuilt and the teaching force restored after the Second World War. New ideas went over the top. 'Child-centred' has thus become a dirty word, so everywhere babies are being thrown out with bath-water. To me, as an observer, the change in primary education was like sepia photographs bursting into colour. We don't want to go back to black and white, just because some of the colour was a bit garish or the definition not always sharp. Indeed, the greatest danger we face is that our primary schools will lose confidence in the very reforms which have brought visitors from all over the world to see them, and will be afraid to stray from the paths that lead to the tests. They will forget that it's beyond the paths that flowers grow, and that many children won't go on any voyage of discovery unless they go with the school. Schools need well-informed ambassadors, parents and governors, who must, if they are to protect the broad curriculum and the process of discovery in delivering it, be allowed near enough to see.

I would think most parents welcome a National Curriculum. Even those who never heard and can't spell the words 'coherence' and 'progression' know the confusion which results when they are missing in any home wanting to support the child's learning. It is like a journey without a map. As for testing, most parents probably welcome some objective information on how their child is progressing in relation to reasonable expectations. But most are appalled by the complexity, rigidity and competitiveness of the testing system as introduced, and would be happier with something more flexible and less stressful. This probably means the use of a bank of standard tests as a means of recording progress, with the teacher in control of timing the tests and communicating results.

Beyond this point parents' understanding of what the government is trying to do to raise standards in education breaks down. There has been so much talk about *choice, competition, information* and *representation*, which are the cornerstones of consumerism, that there will be a terrible day of reckoning if (I am almost brave enough to say 'when') parents find the claims fraudulent.

I return now to the three things I said parents were sure about: the importance of education; the doubt about what is achieved by so much measurement; and the lack of second chances for children.

Education may lead to a job and well-spent leisure. It will also give an as yet unidentified few power over others. It will produce the professionally qualified people who will teach our children and heal our diseases, write our wills and solemnise our marriages. It will nurture creative talent and thereby enrich us all. Is it any wonder that it attracts so many pedlars of dreams who persuade us that there is some magic formula for making it better? A Cinderella's coach in which all can go the ball? An Aladdin's lamp which opens the door to riches for everyone?

Is it any wonder that so many who have the power to change it are schizophrenic; one moment talking about widening the gate of opportunity and then panicking because more seem to be getting through? What else was the reaction to 1992's GCSE results about? What else does it mean when people preach 'relevance' in education from positions of power and influence which they have reached through the great privilege of an irrelevant education, and who are making sure they will still be free to choose the same for their own children? So parents who know how important it is must be sure that the magic potions they are offered will achieve opportunity and not rationing.

The doubt about too much measurement reflects what parents' eyes and ears tell them about schools' needs. While we are so preoccupied with putting the tape measure to schools and children, are we also investing in more and better-trained teachers and the smaller classes which any parent knows to be vital, in books and better-maintained, better-equipped buildings?

Now we come to the fact that children have only one chance. It is this which makes us look hard at the brightly wrapped but perhaps content-free package of *choice, competition, information* and *representation*. I will be daring and say that there is only one of these concepts which has anything to do with better schools for all and that is the last, a wild card which may yet trump the politicians' ace.

Choice? Choice is wonderful. We all want it. In a monopoly service which we are legally obliged to use, it would be folly to say choice doesn't matter and therefore its power to tempt parents away from reality is seductive. If all parents could choose among equally good schools, with equal mobility, confidence, skill, it would be real. It would also be a non-issue, because it is only massive inequality which gives it any meaning. Since there is no plan to invest more in schools (and I don't just mean money) there won't be enough of what parents want to go round, so schools will choose children instead of parents choosing schools. That's rationing.

Competition? I don't think parents accept that children should have to compete for a good education. It should be a right. They may momentarily thrill to the idea of glittering prizes if they think they are going to win, but losing is too terrible to contemplate, whether it's your child or your school.

Information? More information for parents was long overdue.
But all the information prescribed is to help parents choose a school, not to help them be partners in the process. Isn't partnership more important than choice?

Representation? A seat at the table does not guarantee the quality of the meal. But it could, if the system really allowed genuine participation by all classes of the community, the losers as well as the winners, and if the voice crying out for a better-quality meal ever got beyond the table to the kitchen. We must work at this.

Pass and fail. Win or lose. Back the winners, perish the losers. What does it all mean? If you ask that, you are immediately labelled some sloppy radical who wants to protect mediocrity and conceal incompetence.

The most unconvincing feature of the government's programme for raising standards is that if you read it carefully it's all about punishing failure. But isn't it too late when a school's on the skids, bottom of the league table, on the list for the firing squad? Which means too late for somebody's children? Remember, children only have one chance. You can't take them back like a pair of faulty shoes. You can't keep changing schools in a search for the winners without doing untold damage to child and school, even supposing the choice is there.

Parents don't want to make schools accountable for failure. That's too late. They want to ensure that avoidable failure doesn't happen. Yet all the apparatus for spreading good practice, supporting innovation, taking schools and teachers through difficult patches, guiding and advising, is seen as old hat. There isn't a word about it in the government's plans. Only about testing and telling, inspecting and exposing. These processes are cheap, of course - in the very short run. It would be wonderful if there were some magic which could turn all schools into good schools. But most of us know that better schools for all are not so easily won.

LIMITS TO THE AUTONOMOUS SCHOOL:
THE CASE FOR THE LEA OR COMPARABLE BODY

John Tomlinson, Professor of Education, University of Warwick

The reforms in education since 1988, culminating in the proposals of theWhite Paper of 1992, have destroyed the local education authority (LEA). The powers and responsibilities formerly discharged by LEAs have been distributed between central government, school governors and the proposed Schools Funding Agency. What is left after the White Paper is an unrecognisable and probably unworkable rump.

This paper asks 'Does it matter?' The conclusion reached is that it matters a good deal if certain values are deemed important and are to be retained in the education service. These values include: local democratic involvement; the capacity to plan for the future; support and advice to the individual school *besides* what the school may seek and pay for itself; the opportunity to stimulate and carry through innovation which involves many schools and other agencies; and the creation of a local focus to which parents can turn which is *not* the school, not the finance-driven Schools Funding Agency and not central government distant in Whitehall.

1. Local democratic accountability

The LEAs were created in 1902 and given additional responsibilities in 1944 and thereafter because they were embedded in local government and therefore accountable through the ballot box. They were seen as the engine by which broad national policy could be adapted to local conditions and aspirations within a framework of local control. Officials could be held directly and locally accountable, and councillors could be turned out at election time. The LEA also formed part of a deliberately chosen constitutional framework for the distribution of power. Until recently, few in this country have wanted to see control of education entirely put in the hands of central government.

The experience of pre-First World War Germany and of fascist states between the wars created a cross-party determination not to concentrate power at one level of government.

The rapid and continuous removal of powers from the LEAs during the 1980s has been justified, on the few occasions when it has been admitted and argued at all, on some or all of the following grounds:

- the need to acknowledge that we are a small nation state, as seen in the context of Europe, and must garner the capacity to govern into one place

- the inability of LEAs effectively to economise in finance over surplus school places

- the party political extremism of some LEAs

- the virtual irrelevance of the LEA once grant-maintained schools become the norm.

It is not clear that any of these arguments, to the extent that they can be justified, would remove the fundamental case for an element of local democratic control and accountability in the education service. The truth is that the argument has never been put into the public domain for discussion and decision either in the popular sense or through Parliamentary debate. The changes, fundamental to our constitution though they are, have been made piecemeal and pragmatically. The principles remain unexamined.

2. Admissions to schools; and support and advice to schools

The vision on offer after 1988 and the White Paper of 1992 is of 25,000 virtually autonomous schools operating as a market place. They hire the teachers, buy what services they deem necessary, and receive money from the Schools Funding Agency according to the number of pupils they have attracted and a formula laid down by the Secretary of State. Four-yearly inspections will both help inform parents and identify failing schools which, if failings persist, will then be taken over by an education association.

There are two problems with this view of schooling which relate to the historic functions of LEAs.

Admissions

Parental requests for their children to enter particular schools in an order of preference need to be organised and processed at a scale larger than any individual school and according to some public criteria of fairness.   In fact, the right of each governing body to choose both removes parental rights of choice where popular schools are concerned and can create delay and uncertainty as decisions are made unsystematically. The question is simply whether principles of equity and good order are any longer to be regarded as important. If they are, then some LEA-style function will be needed.

Advice and support

It is a mistake to think that people always know what they need. The system now on offer will encourage schools to buy the advice and support they *want*. It may not be what they need. In those LEAs where inspection, advice and support have been sensitively and successfully organised, it has been possible for LEA advisers to work with a school on both diagnosing need and effecting remedies.

Schools usually have failings or potential failings in specific areas

- a curriculum subject
- an aspect of management or pastoral care
- in relationships with parents or industry.

A mature relationship of scrutiny and criticism by school and LEA working regularly together can both diagnose such failings in good time and set in hand remedial work to put them right and improve the whole body politic of a school in the process. The White Paper offers instead the notion of total school failure, a '*big bang*', publicly and dramatically acknowledged by the four-yearly inspection, after which an education association would move in. It is a totally inappropriate way of conceptualising school improvement except in the most rare and pathological cases. Yet once the Schools Funding Agency has taken over LEA functions, the alternative of help-on-the-hoof will not be available.

3. Innovation

At their best, LEAs have been the well-spring of innovation. Most of the valuable innovation of this century has come from LEA/school action. I would cite as examples middle schools, training in management for heads and senior staff, schools as cost centres, school-based curriculum development and evaluation, curriculum-based staffing, records of achievement, residential curriculum centres, outdoor education centres, teachers' centres, the schools psychological service, education/industry liaison, community education, and much else. All the lessons from experience suggest that innovation, even though it may be stimulated nationally, needs grass-rooted involvement to succeed. Where will the local networks be? The LEA has hitherto offered a ready-made vehicle. The Funding Agency would not be equipped to provide them. If they are to be set up specifically for every new development, the cost would be appalling and no doubt prohibitive.

4. Planning for the future

The notion that a market/in schools driven by governing bodies which may propose to expand or contract or set up new schools according to popularity and demographic change seems a frail vehicle through which to ensure that sufficient school places are available and in the right places to meet the needs of communities as they change. The local authority has the knowledge and capacity through its planning, housing and other functions to scan the future and create sensible development plans for educational provision. It seems ludicrous that this capacity should not in the future continue to be used.

5. Conclusion

The residual role envisaged for the LEA in the White Paper, of provider of special education and some pupil-specific services, is deeply unsatisfactory when judged against the record of LEAs, the values of local community and accountability, the capacity for innovation and improvement demonstrated by LEAs, and the need to provide a point of contact for parents which is independent of any particular school.

Let a considerable group of parents have the last word:

> *'Area Federations of NCPTA do not support the Government's belief that Grant Maintained Status is the answer which will solve all that is claimed to be wrong with the present Education system. Within the proposals contained in the Paper 'Choice and Diversity, A Framework for Schools', we see:*

> - *an increase in bureaucratic control*
> - *a diminution of local democracy*
> - *an increase in the power of the State*
> - *parental 'choice' being reduced and cheque book led*
> - a misleading use of the words 'parental choice'.

> *A parent of primary school age children involved in the preparation of this response observed that she had a great fear. As a Governor, the powers and responsibilities she will be asked to take on will increase but without the experience, knowledge and assistance of the LEA, which is an essential life raft. There will be new bureaucratic bodies centrally and regionally with little local knowledge. She is very concerned; to whom*

*will parents turn when they face problems at the local school? She is very
worried that when problems arise there will be no local democratic route
to take.*

*LEAs will always have a role to play in helping parents. Teachers will
continue to need the professional advice, support and guidance presently
available within the Local Education Authority. Therefore we ask that
some ongoing provisions be made.'*

> *(response to the DFE White Paper by Area Federations of the NCPTA,
> September 1992)*

The conclusion presses in that we ought not to allow ourselves to be led into
a system which relies on the individual school backed by a central funding
agency without a careful examination of the merits of having an intermediate
competent in education development, forward planning and the resolution of
conflict. The regional office of the School Funding Agency and the
drastically circumscribed LEA, which are all that is on offer, do not provide
that essential function.

Further reading by John Tomlinson

- *The Control of Education.* Cassell. 1993.

TRADITIONAL OR PROGRESSIVE:
IS THERE REALLY A CHOICE?

Philip Waterhouse, Former Headteacher,
Leading Authority on Teaching and Learning Styles

Prizes for the 1992 vogue words in education must surely go to 'traditional' and 'progressive'. And lay people can hardly be blamed for assuming that they are presented with a stark choice; they must choose one or the other. Unfortunately the two words all too easily conjure up very clear images.

On the one hand, 'traditional' teaching suggests a formal atmosphere, whole-class teaching, and a didactic style. There is an emphasis on correct procedures, on discipline, and on precisely defined relationships between teacher and taught. The members of the class, for the most part, work on the same things at the same time. They spend most of their time under the close control of the teacher, who determines the subject content and how the work is to be tackled. The teacher's stimulus, guidance and instructions form the pivot around which each lesson revolves.

On the other hand, 'progressive' teaching suggests a more informal atmosphere, much individual and small-group work, and a collaborative style. Discussion, negotiation and choice play a larger part. Much work is done individually or in small groups. Students move about the classroom according to the needs of the task in hand. The teacher often works with individuals, or small groups.

The current fashion is to argue that progressive methods do not work and that standards will be raised by a return to the traditional.

It is so easy to get carried away. Most of us remember at least one good traditional teacher - a strong, determined personality, knowledgeable, highly articulate, and often with a tremendous wit. The students were expected to conform and to relate only to the teacher's leadership, but this didn't seem to be too burdensome considering the lively and purposeful atmosphere. Many such teachers are remembered with affection.

But most of us will also remember teachers who, while keeping a tight traditional control on the discipline of the classroom, failed to challenge or stimulate their students. Their lessons were a dreary trudge through uninspiring routines and a monotonous recitation of colourless information and inert ideas.

The content of the lessons passed from the teacher's lesson notes into the students' notebooks without passing through the heads of either of them. Frequently these teachers have defended the 'traditional' approach and have been the most vehement opponents of 'progressive' methods. Yet they themselves have been the main target of the strongest criticisms of teaching made by Her Majesty's Inspectors of Schools in recent years.

In progressive teaching there are also the successes and the failures. It is the failures that have attracted some publicity. These are teachers whose attitude and work are driven by convictions that are more sociological and political than educational. They believe in choice and freedom, in spontaneity and autonomy for the student. But they extend these basic ideas into a rejection of structure and prescription which leads them to a wholesale condemnation of traditional forms of teaching and a weak 'laissez-faire' philosophy. Their classrooms are often disorganised and disorderly, and the chaos is justified with vague assertions about student autonomy. Fortunately, most experienced observers of our schools will affirm that these teachers are a very small minority.

So where does this leave the bulk of the teaching profession? It needs stating most firmly that the vast majority of teachers do not belong to the 'looney progressives' who have been the favourite target of some commentators. Most teachers in today's schools lean towards a cautious and fairly traditional stance. They believe in a firm but fair disciplinary framework with a well-structured approach to learning through clearly set targets and carefully designed activities and experiences. They believe that much of this can be accomplished in whole-class traditional teaching (as our example of the good traditional teacher has shown). But many of them are not content to leave the matter there. They believe that a sole addiction to whole-class didactic teaching often takes away student initiative and responsibility, leaving students inadequately prepared for their continuing education and for adult life. So they want to extend their teaching repertoires to include some individual and small-group work. They do this through a strong emphasis on objectives, on responsibility and answerability. Their students do not find these new approaches a soft option, and many have testified to the fact that these arrangements often lead to higher levels of motivation and increased commitment to work.

So categorising and labelling teachers as 'progressive' or 'traditional' is confusing and pointless.

The teachers themselves do not want it and it gives a false picture to parents and the community in general. Instead we should focus quite simply on the good teaching that can produce high-level academic achievements and at the same time prepare young people for the demands of adult life. This good teaching demands extraordinary versatility on the part of the teacher. The really good teacher is capable of inspiring and leading a class in the traditional mode. Students appreciate this and such lessons can be highly motivating. But that teacher is also equally capable of managing a classroom in a different mode, in which the teacher takes on new roles as manager, tutor and counsellor. This involves a range of quite different activities. The class is often organised into small groups, and the teacher's work is in helping students to accept and define their own learning objectives, showing them how to improve the quality of their learning through small-group discussions and tutorials. It is more difficult to organise than a traditional whole-class lesson. But with the support of some of the recent development work in classroom practice, more and more teachers feel themselves to be equipped to extend their repertoires in these directions. They are not replacing class teaching; they are diversifying and enriching, but cautiously.

It should be cause for optimism that, even in these difficult times, more and more teachers are, in carefully controlled ways, extending the range of their own personal teaching styles. Mistakes are sometimes made because classrooms are notoriously complex places, but that is how experience is acquired and mistakes can be easily rectified. These teachers are convinced that the education that we give to our young people must be improved. But they know that the simplistic categorisation into 'traditional' and 'progressive' makes no useful contribution. They just need some appreciation and encouragement, backed by a continuation of some of the research, development and training initiatives which have helped them so much in recent years.

Further reading by Philip Waterhouse

- *Flexible Learning: An Outline.* Network Educational Press. 1990.
- *Classroom Management.* Network Educational Press. 1990.
- *Tutoring.* Network Educational Press. 1991.

PRIMARY EDUCATION

Ted Wragg, Professor of Education, Exeter University

Primary education has received a bad press during the last few years.
Visitors to this country cannot understand why what they actually see in
classrooms does not square with what they have read in newspapers. They
expect to witness failure, yet they usually come away impressed with most, if
not all, of what they have seen.

A sustained campaign in the popular press has told the public that standards
are falling. Yet the analysis of maths test scores of pupils-aged 11 undertaken
by the Assessment of Performance Unit from 1984 to 1988 showed that
achievement had improved in four out of the five aspects of mathematics
tested; namely, measures, algebra, probability/statistics and geometry.
However, in the fifth area, that of number, scores had indeed gone down.
This is a matter of concern, given the prominence of number work in adult
life and the importance it holds in public perception, but the overall results
do not demonstrate poorer maths teaching generally.

Teachers' professional skills

I have analysed the observations of over a thousand lessons as part of the
Leverhulme Primary Project at Exeter University. We studied teaching in
the North and the South, in city and country schools, in the classrooms of
beginners, and experienced and supply teachers. We also interviewed
both teachers and pupils. The results were not in accord with the popular
picture of indiscipline and poor achievement.

One of the studies we undertook was of the very first days of the school
year, those vital first encounters in September when the climate is set for the
rest of the session. Most teachers used a firm but friendly approach, and
were quick to establish and reinforce rules, and we saw very little
misbehaviour. In assemblies children were exhorted to behave well, to set
a good example and to be thoughtful about others. Studies we undertook
later in the school year showed that the most common form of misbehaviour
was noisy or illicit chatter, rather than aggression, damage to property or
insults to the teacher, all of which were relatively rare.

There were, of course, some exceptions to this general orderliness, though
they were in the minority. In one urban school two teachers in adjacent
classrooms were quite different from each other, the one experiencing

misbehaviour and a high degree of chaos, the other running a well-behaved and industrious classroom. The former, however, was inconsistent in her application of rules, and pupils had to explore the limits to find out what they were. The latter was good-humoured and had high expectations, was consistent in her rule enforcements and was well liked by the children. Neither teacher fitted any crude 'traditional' or 'progressive' stereotype, however: it was much more subtle than that. It was the craft of the classroom that was different, not the ideology.

When we looked at teachers' professional skills, such as explaining or questioning, a similar picture of competence emerged. Asked to explain a topic like 'Insects' to 8 or 9-year-olds, most teachers demonstrated considerable proficiency, successfully teaching children to distinguish insects from other similar animals and understand the essential characteristics of the creatures and their way of life. Only a few communicated poorly, either because they made a bad choice of words or examples, lacked clarity, or did not possess sufficient factual knowledge themselves.

On the matter of questioning the picture was more mixed. Relatively few of the questions asked by teachers we observed required more than the recall of factual information, and most were to do with the management of the lesson. There is no research evidence that asking higher-order questions which require children to analyse, evaluate, make inferences or use their imagination is any better than asking a string of factual recall questions, but I would personally have liked to see more of these than the 8% we actually observed. None the less there were several examples of challenging and thought-provoking sequences of questions.

Subject knowledge

One of the most difficult problems facing primary teachers in the late twentieth century is the considerable amount of subject knowledge they are expected to possess. The introduction of a National Curriculum in the 1988 Education Act put heavy demands on teachers to master the content in nine very large subject areas. Lock a set of nine separate groups of enthusiasts away for several weeks, asking them to devise a syllabus in their own subject, and each will come back with something requiring half the week.

History for 7 to 11-year-olds covers all the invaders and settlers from the Romans to the last busload of tourists, the Tudors and Stuarts, the routes to the Spice Islands, the building technology of the Pyramids and the Parthenon, the Aztecs and a host of other topics about which most of us know precious little. Alongside needing to know about the history of plough design, primary teachers are expected to know all the science syllabus, including physical science topics such as 'electricity and magnetism' or 'forces', biology themes like 'genetics' or 'the processes of life', and also master Earth sciences, astronomy and climatology.

In a survey of more than 1,300 primary teachers we found that English and maths were the only two subjects where teachers felt able to teach the National Curriculum without much assistance. In technology, where confidence was lowest, only one in seven teachers felt competent to cover the vast syllabus (embracing business studies and home economics, as well as craft skills, design and evaluation) without extra help. Yet primary teachers, overwhelmed as they are by the subject demands in nine huge areas of expertise, have been given virtually no time at all to study these subjects for themselves, as full-time secondments for teachers virtually disappeared when local management of schools was introduced and the central cash fund, which underwrote teacher release, was closed down.

The real killer for teachers is not so much preparing lessons, something most do assiduously in subjects they do not know well, as coping with children's questions. Why does most sand sink in water, but some grains float? Why does an orange float when whole, but sink when you peel it? Or, in the words of one 7-year-old in a class I was teaching, 'Why does a wagtail wag its tail?' In the circumstances, teachers desperately need people who can help them with advice about the relevant scientific concepts, as well as with appropriate strategies and materials, yet teachers' centres and advisory posts are being closed down.

The future of primary schooling

In many ways good primary schools prepare children extremely well for the twenty-first century. Alvin Toffler said that all education is a vision of the future, and predictions for the twenty first century suggest that many people will work in service jobs, rather than on factory production lines, that a high level of skill will be needed in both home and working life, that people may re-train several times, and that many human and scientific problems will be solved by teams rather than individuals. At its best, primary education prepares children well to be flexible, skilful, imaginative and to work as a member of a collaborative team.

I see three major needs for the future. The first is for a different kind of national curriculum at the primary stage. A nine-subject curriculum for 5-year-olds makes no sense. Most other countries have opted for fewer.

I would advocate a huge attack on basic literacy as soon as children arrive in school, so that they are in a position, as soon as possible, to commence autonomous learning. This should be accompanied not by eight academic subjects, but by fewer 'domains', such as 'numeracy', 'the arts', including movement and dance, what the Germans call '*Heimatkunde*' or '*knowledge of your own backyard*', be that town or village, and a 'how the world works' approach to science and technology. This kind of curriculum would permit direct instruction and sound topic, project and practical work.

Secondly, I would reform and simplify the National Curriculum for 7 to 11-year-olds. Most countries have their national curriculum in a single pamphlet. We alone have shelves full of detailed prescription. Small wonder that the testing-led model of the curriculum, with its emphasis on discrete, testable micro-objectives, has buried teachers under its own self-perpetuating bureaucracy. Some sacrifice in breadth would be more than compensated for by gains in depth. There should be no clamour, however, for losing the gains in the National Curriculum, notably the real improvement, despite the problems, in the teaching of the physical sciences and technology in the junior school. Furthermore, the taboo which some have placed on having a degree of specialist teaching in the upper years of primary education seems to me mistaken. It is perfectly possible to preserve the 'class teacher' notion and still offer children access to the expertise of semi-specialist colleagues.

Thirdly, I would like to see a sustained programme of higher horizons and expectations from primary pupils. For fear of expecting too much it is easy to expect too little. The most impressive primary teachers I see have high, but realistic, expectations, which they achieve in a benign and imaginative manner.

In public opinion surveys three-quarters of parents think standards are falling, yet three-quarters or more are satisfied with their own child's school. It seems an odd paradox until you realise that they think standards must be falling elsewhere, because of the unfairly hostile press which primary schools receive. Primary schools, whilst not perfect, are in practice far more impressive than the public has been led to believe.

Further reading by Ted Wragg

- *Class Management.*
- *Questioning.*
- *Explaining.*
- *Primary Teaching Skills.*

All to be published by Routledge 1993.

NETWORK EDUCATIONAL PRESS
FURTHER PUBLICATIONS

The Teaching and Learning Series

What Makes a Good School?   Tim Brighouse

- What makes a good teacher?
- What creates a successful environment?
- How can schools review for success?
- How can leaders raise staff morale?

Tim Brighouse, former Chief Education Officer for Oxfordshire and now Professor of Education at Keele University uses his vast experience to answer these key questions. His insights into school life - both the good and the bad - are topical, relevant and entertaining.

ISBN 1 85539 007 8   £6.50

Other books in the Teaching and Learning Series

Flexible Learning: An Outline   Philip Waterhouse
ISBN 1 85539 003 5   £6.50

Classroom Management   Philip Waterhouse
ISBN 1 85539 004 3   £6.50

Resources for Flexible Learning   Robert Powell
ISBN 1 85539 005 1   £6.50

Tutoring   Philip Waterhouse
ISBN 1 85539 006 X   £6.50

All publications available from:
Network Educational Press Ltd, PO Box 635, Stafford, ST17 0JR
Telephone 0785 225515